Faith that Transcends

A Study Guide for the Letter to the Hebrews

Steven P. Thomason
Vibble Books

Faith that Transcends

by
Steven P. Thomason

Published by:

Vibble Books

www.VibbleBooks.com

All rights reserved. No part of this book may be reproduced or transmitted in any form or by any means, electronic or mechanical, including photocopying, recording or by any information storage and retrieval system without written permission from the author.

Scripture quotations marked (NIV) are taken from the HOLY BIBLE, NEW INTERNATIONAL VERSION®. NIV®. Copyright© 1973, 1978, 1984 by International Bible Society. Used by permission of Zondervan.

All rights reserved.

Copyright © 2009 Steven P. Thomason

ISBN: 0-9840670-5-1
13-Digit: 978-0-9840670-5-3

Cover Artwork and Interior Illustration: Steven P. Thomason

Printed in the United States of America

Table of Contents

Master Illustration iv

Introduction 1

Lesson 1: Jesus is Above the Angels 5

Lesson 2: Jesus Went Below the Angels
to Become Our Brother 11

Lesson 3: Jesus is Greater than Moses 21

Lesson 4: The Deep Sabbath 27

Lesson 5: Jesus is a Better High Priest 35

Lesson 6: Grow Up and Hang On! 41

Lesson 7: Jesus is a Priest Like Melchizedek 49

Lesson 8: A New Tent and Promise 57

Lesson 9: Parables of Heaven 65

Lesson 10: More Salad 75

Lesson 11: The Story of Faith 85

Lesson 12: Running the Race 97

Lesson 13: Going Outside the City 109

Master Illustration

Vibble Books is committed to the needs of the visual learner. This illustration is designed to capture the essence of the message found in Hebrews in one image. To view the full color, interactive version, visit the Vibble online at *www.vibblespace.com/Hebrews*

HEBREWS

Introduction

The Message of Hebrews is both the easiest and the most difficult to understand of all the New Testament books. In order to save you some frustration and the possibility of having your head spin from cultural whiplash, let's begin with the easiest understanding. Simply put, the letter to the Hebrews says,

Jesus is superior to the "Old School" ideas of Judaism. You can trust Jesus completely, so don't cave in under persecution; stay strong and don't give up!

That's pretty easy to grasp. At this point you may be tempted to say, "I get that, I believe it, why don't we just skip the confusing stuff and call it good." For some people that might actually be a good option. However, let me encourage you to take the plunge into this wonderfully complex and culturally thick letter. There are two reasons why this will be a beneficial study for you:

1. Through this study you will gain a deeper understanding of the Jewish mindset that was dominant in the world of Jesus, the apostles, and the writing of the New Testament. It is impossible to fully grasp the original intent of the New Testament without having a working knowledge of this 1st century Jewish perspective. Thus, by developing a richer understanding of it you will, in turn, be increasing your ability to correctly interpret the rest of the New Testament. That's always a good thing.

2. Even more important than becoming a better student of the New Testament, the study of this book will undoubtedly shed new light on the nature of Jesus. In every paragraph of this document Jesus is exalted as the pinnacle of all creation. Few other passages of the New Testament pay Jesus higher respect than Hebrews. As you soak in this authors' words, and as you let the Holy Spirit soak these words into you, new vistas of understanding regarding the purpose of Jesus' life, teaching, death, and resurrection will unfold before you and the potential for your faith to be deepened in His role as "Commander and Chief" of the universe will increase. Once again, a very positive reason.

Now, let's dive into the aspects of Hebrews that makes its message difficult to understand. It is difficult because it is Jewish. That is not to say anything negative about being Jewish; by no means. If you were a Jew in the first century Hebrews would simply be a long string of enlightening "aha" moments. The author masterfully argues from the Jewish worldview how it is obvious and a logical outflow of the trajectory of the Hebrew Scripture and Theology that Jesus is the Messiah who has brought with Him a New World Order. The reason it is difficult is because you, if my assumptions are correct, are most likely not a 1st century Jew. Chances are you are a 21st century, Protestant, middle-class, American who knows very little about the theology of the Old Testament, let alone the complex Jewish theology that was constructed during the 400 years period of time between the end of the Old Testament and the beginning of the New Testament.

At this point we have two options. The first option would be to spew out reams of information that would ground you in the context of 1st century Judaism. Or, similarly, we could all enroll in a post-graduate course on the subject in a seminary. While a small fraction of the population might find that appealing, the chances are that you would bolt for the door at the first sign of something like that. Don't worry. We're not going down that path. The first and most fundamental reason we aren't going that direction is because I (being a 21st century, middle-class, Protestant, American, not having a Ph.D. in 1st century Judaism) could not write something like that, and, secondly, it would be better to touch on pertinent issues along the way as we work our way through the text.

That leaves us with our second option. For introduction to the letter we will state some simple facts about the Author, Audience, and Setting for the book.

Author: We don't know. Traditionally this book has been attributed to Paul, but there is just too much about it that is so vastly different from anything else he wrote that it was probably not written by him. However, it is an example of the kind of logical thought-processes he probably went through as he "reasoned from the scriptures" with the Jews in the synagogues during his journeys in Acts. As to who wrote the book, there are some educated guesses, but no definitive conclusions. The Greek style of the letter betrays the fact the author was very well educated and a master at a style of communication that is called Greek Rhetorical Argumentation. In light of this it is possible that Apollos is the author. We meet him in Acts 18. He came from Alexandria, Egypt (the mother ship for the Rhetorical Tradition), was a Jew, and was as well respected among the early church as Paul. Some people say it was written by others such as Luke, Silas, and even Priscilla (wouldn't that be wonderfully scandalous if the author was actually a woman!) Suffice it to say that the author was a

HEBREWS

highly educated and well respected pastor who had a passionate message to deliver.

Audience: It is obvious from the moment you begin reading that the audience is Jewish. However, given the excellent Greek style, the use of the Greek Rhetorical Tradition, and the reference to the Greek translation of the Hebrew Scriptures (called the Septuagint) it is most likely that these Jews were Greek speaking Jews that lived in a place (or places) far away from Israel. These "Hellenized" Jews (meaning Jews that had adapted to Greek culture) had been "dispersed" throughout the Roman Empire for centuries. They lived in the constant tension between their strong cultural heritage and belief in God's special relationship with the nation of Israel expressed through the Law of Moses and the reality that they lived in and among pagan gentiles that ruled the universe. As Hellenized Jews that had acknowledged Jesus to be the prophesied Messiah and the supreme ruler of the universe (over and above the Roman Emperor) they faced even greater tension. This tension reached a zenith as they had popped up on the Roman Empire's radar as a threat to Roman peace. Under the rule of Nero the followers of Jesus had become scapegoats for the partly crazed Emperor's narcissistic shortcomings and had experienced severe and ruthless persecution. Not only were the Romans antagonistic toward "Christians" (a derogatory term in those days) they were also fed up with the constant turmoil in Judea and had launched a war against the Jews to silence them once and for all. So, no matter where these Hellenistic Jewish Christians turned, they faced imminent danger.

Date: Given the mention of Timothy's release in chapter 13 and the absence of the mention of Paul, as well as having no mention of the destruction of the temple, it is a good guess to date the writing of this letter between AD 64 (when Paul died) and AD 70 (when the Romans destroyed the temple). By AD 68 the Romans were very confident that they would defeat the Jews and wreak great destruction on them, so it was easy to see why the author of Hebrews could refer to the Temple rituals as "passing away."

Setting: Hebrews was written to Jewish Christians who were sitting on the fence. They were teetering on the edge of betraying their faith. The Romans were forcing the Christians to make a choice: either denounce Jesus as Lord, pay homage to Caesar as Divine Ruler, pay taxes and make sacrifices to him OR face the confiscation of all property, the imprisonment of the entire household, torture, and possible death. What would you do? If someone held a gun to your head, or worse yet, to your young daughter's head, would you hold your ground? Or, would you rationalize in your mind that you could say what they wanted to hear in order to save your own skin or your family's lives and property? It's a painful reality that most of us have never faced. Yet, that was the dilemma facing the recipients of this letter.

It is important for us to keep this violent reality in our minds as we read the letter. The ideas presented in this letter are not the abstract theological constructions of a heady theologian who has a cushy teaching job in a prestigious seminary with a view of the ocean. These are the words of a brilliant and passionate pastor who knew that everything hung in the balance for these Christians (and even for himself). On the one side the Romans are hounding them to cave in. On the other hand the elders of the synagogue are trying to convince them that belief in Jesus as the Messiah is heresy and is the reason for the persecution and potential destruction of Jerusalem. Their Jewish family, friends, and neighbors are urging them to return to an adherence to the Laws and the rituals of the temple...before it is too late. The author knew that if they turned to the right or to the left they may forever cut off the flow of Jesus' grace and mercy that they had so recently and abundantly received. Their only hope is to look past the constructs of man and the "shadowy representations of Reality" that are found in the Law and keep their eyes on Jesus who is the "author and perfector" the "starter and finisher" of their faith. They must cling to Him and trust in His reality so that they can stay strong and live in the reality of Jesus' Kingdom both now and for eternity. As we read through these pages may our awareness of the things that distract us from Jesus become heightened and may our tenacious trust in the reality of Jesus' Lordship and Grace be strengthened to our core.

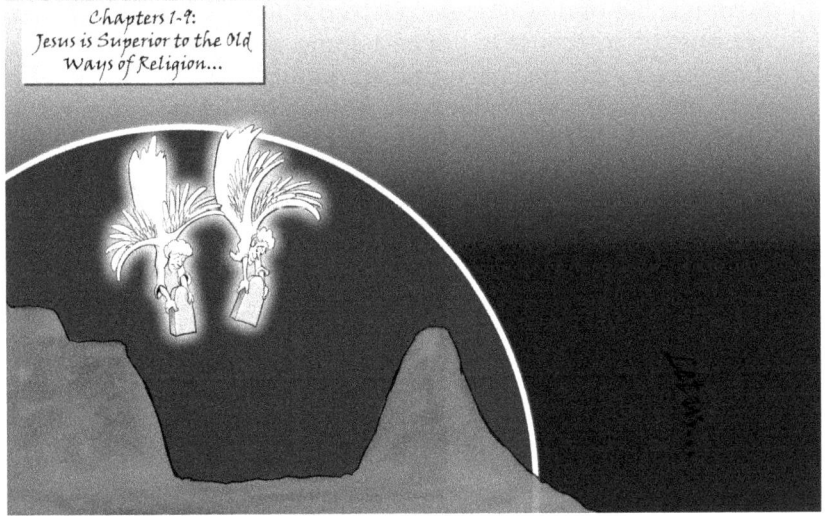

Lesson 1: Jesus Is Above the Angels

- Read: Hebrews 1

Study Questions

1. In what way is God's communication similar and different between the way He communicated "in the past" and "in these last days?"

2. Make a list of the ways the Son is described in verses 2-4. As you contemplate this list what emotional response do you have to it? What questions does it raise for you?

Faith that Transcends

3. Here is a list of all the passages from the Old Testament that are quoted in this text. Spend some time reading through these texts and the surrounding passage from which they were extracted. How does the author of Hebrews interpret these texts? What response or questions does this raise for you?

    Psalm 2:7

    2 Samuel 7:14

    Psalm 104:4

    Psalm 45:6-7

    Psalm 102:25-27

    Psalm 110:1

4. In what way is the Son compared to angels? Why do you think the author emphasizes this point?

HEBREWS

Food for Thought

1-4 Setting the Bar

In this introduction the author establishes the basic premise of the entire message. Jesus is supreme. Jesus is not just a great teacher or a moral example for how to live. Yes, He is those things, but He is so much more. Jesus is God's Son, the heir of all God's glory, He is the exact representation of the substance of God. In other words, He is God. Jesus is not just Godlike, nor is He the most wonderfully created thing. He is God, the creator and sustainer of all matter in the universe. When you look to Jesus you are looking at the source and continuing force of your very being. In Him you can put your confidence.

There. Now that the author has established his main point he will proceed to demonstrate it by comparing Jesus to all the things that the Jewish culture had heretofore upheld as the most exalted and reliable things in the universe. Jesus is greater than angels, than Moses, than the Law, than the Tabernacle, than the blood of sacrifice, and the covenant itself. In Jesus all these things have been fulfilled, surpassed, and conflated so that He can establish a New Covenant that is able to free the world from the power of sin and empower us to enter into God's presence without fear or regret.

5-14 Jesus is Superior to Angels

So what's all this about angels?

During the period of time between the destruction of Jerusalem in 586 BC and the life of Jesus, the Jewish theology of angels became very elaborate and very integral to their spirituality. The Jews believed (as did all the ancient societies) that God lived high up in the Heavens, beyond the reach of man. In between God and man was "the Heavens," the spiritual realm where beings called angels lived, moving back and forth between Heaven and Earth. Some of these angels were good and some were bad. On both sides of the equation the angels were highly organized into hierarchical ranks, much like our modern military. The "host" of angels were led by the archangels who stood at the top of the heap and in the presence of God. Below them were myriad of angels, each with their own assignments. Some were messengers, some were avengers, some were protectors of children, others were like lawyers who stood in God's Heavenly court and either accused or defended humans.

There are two important factors regarding the Jewish belief about angels that pertains to our study of Hebrews.

1. They believed that angels were a necessary intermediary between God and Man. Without them we could not have access to God. They were the highest form of created being in the universe and were intrinsically related to God's glory.
2. In light of #1, they believed that the Law of Moses was given to him by angels, since they served as the intermediary between God and man.

It is important to point out that this theology was not derived from scripture. The Old Testament definitely refers to angels and spirits, but it stops at reference. It never elaborates on the nature of the spiritual beings nor their organizational structure. All of that theology comes from two sources. First, there are books called the Apocrypha which were written during the centuries between Old and New Testament that go into much more detail about these topics. The Apocryphal books were not regarded as scripture by the Jews. The second source (which some believe was actually the source for the Apocryphal books) is the influence of Persian religion that the Jews experienced during their exile. Zoroastrianism was a strong religious force in Persia and it taught about a staircase that stretched between God and man upon which angels and demons fought for human passage.

How should we think about angels?

There are three options for how we should think about angels today, as followers of Jesus and students of the Bible:

Option #1

The Spiritual world is exactly like the ancient Jews described it. There is a literal army of Good Angels under the leadership of archangels and there is a literal army of Bad Angels under the leadership of Satan. Everyday they battle for our minds and fill the gap between us and God.

Option #2

The terms "angels" and "demons" come from an ancient worldview and are simply a concrete metaphor representing physical phenomenon that transcends human understanding. In our modern/post-modern context we need to abandon the ancient terms and find new language and metaphors that will help us communicate our interaction with the mysteries of the universe.

Option #3

A combination of #1 & #2. Notice that neither 1 or 2 denied a spiritual reality. Both acknowledge a deep gap between the spiritual reality of God's existence and our own material existence. The fact is that scripture itself does not elaborate on the details of the spiritual world. We don't need to abandon the terms, but we should be open to better ways of understanding the nature of the spiritual realit

So what's the point in Hebrews?

The author of Hebrews was speaking to an audience that was thoroughly entrenched in Option #1. The scandal of Jesus is that He claimed to be above and beyond the angels. The angels are not the intermediary between God and man, Jesus is. Jesus is not the highest form of creation that stands in the glory of God, Jesus is the character and substance of God, the creator of all things and through Him we have direct access to God, no angels needed.

To be a Jew who decided to follow Jesus meant more than just acknowledging Jesus as the Messiah. It required some massive deconstruction of distorted theologies that had bubbled up over the centuries. This is a very painful process to go through. It also creates great strife within a cultural and family system. "What do you mean you don't need to go through your guardian angel? What kind of heresy is this? No child of mine is going to speak such nonsense!!" You can just imagine what the families and synagogues gossiped about when little Josiah decided to follow Jesus as the Messiah! The author of Hebrews was calling for his audience to resist the temptation to be drawn back into this distorted theology.

Faith that Transcends

Now we need to come to our time. What does any of this have to do with us? There are some very important transferable principles for the life of a Jesus-follower today. The reality is that whenever we talk about God, sin, salvation, and the spiritual world, we are treading into waters that are deep and mysterious. There are realities in the universe that are beyond our comprehension. It is the human tendency to construct ideas that tame these deep mysteries, explain them, put them in a box, and make them serve us. Even if the thing we have created is a tyrannical god that demands horrible things from us it is still a defined reality that we can grasp. It's like the battered wife who would rather stay with the known pain of abuse than to venture into the realm of the unknown. In light of this, there are many "Christian Doctrines" about the spiritual world that exist and compete with each other in our world today. Many of these belief systems flow right from the Jewish mysticism we have been discussing in this lesson. Here's the point from Hebrews 1: Jesus is above and beyond all that. Jesus is the Son of God who supercedes the need for spiritual intermediaries. He is not dependent upon the angels to deliver His grace and mercy, nor is He in the same category as them. As we will see throughout the development of Hebrews, Jesus has created a new order for us. He has made things very simple. He gave us direct access to God. We don't need superstitious fear of spirit beings (even if they are a reality, we need not fear them), we don't need ritualistic sacrifice of animals, we don't need a fear-based adherence to a legal code. We simply need Jesus, the high priest, the Son of God, the lover of our souls.

As you move into this week, rest in the assurance that Jesus is all you need. Don't become distracted by extraneous theologies and philosophies that confuse you and draw your attention from the reality that Jesus is the Lord of all things and that He welcomes you into God's presence. I realize that concept in itself is a deep mystery that can be nearly impossible to explain. The beauty is that we don't have to explain it to believe it any more than we need to explain the pulmonary system to be able to breath. Jesus is the air we breathe, so take it in and be free from fear and be freed to love.

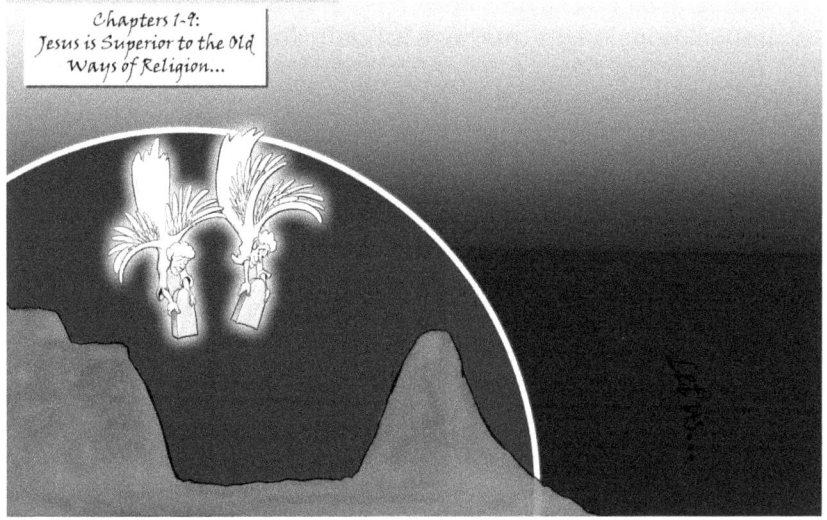

Lesson 2: Jesus Went Below the Angels to Become Our Brother

- Read: Hebrews 2

Study Questions

1. What is the author's purpose for writing these things? (verse 1)

2. How was "this salvation" confirmed? Where do we find this documented in the New Testament?

3. To whom has God subjected the world to come? To whom has it not been subjected? Why do you think this point may have been emphasized?

Faith that Transcends

4. In verses 8-9, how is Jesus' rule (the fact that everything has been subjected to Him) described in the present time? What implications might this have for daily life?

5. Why did Jesus have to die?

6. Verse 12 is a quote from Psalm 22. Read Psalm 22. When you realize that this is one of the Psalms that Jesus quoted while hanging on the cross, how does it impact your understanding of this part of Hebrews 2?

7. Verse 13 is a quote from Isaiah 8. What is the historical context of Isaiah 8 (in other words, what's going on in the nation that is influencing Isaiah's writing)? What analogies might Hebrews be trying to make between the current circumstances and the situation in Isaiah 8?

HEBREWS

8. What effect did Jesus' death have for humanity?

9. What is Jesus' relationship to humanity? How and Why?

10. What new image of Jesus is introduced in verse 17? What relevance might this have had to the original reader?

11. How was Jesus tempted? What correlation might there be between Jesus' temptation and the situation of the audience of Hebrews?

Faith that Transcends

Food for Thought

1-4 Since He is Higher than the Angels, His Message is Better than Theirs

Here are some important points to keep in mind:

1. The Jews believed that angels ruled over the places of the earth. They essentially filled the Heavens (the space between God and humanity). These angels were good and evil and battled for dominance.
2. The Jews believed that angels delivered the Law to Moses on Mt. Sinai, therefore associated the Law of Moses with angels. Thus, the phrase "the message spoken by angels" in verse 2 is to be understood as the Law of Moses.

In light of the above points, we can paraphrase this section as follows:

> *If the Law of Moses was important, and God punished people who wandered away from it, then the message that Jesus brought is even more important and more serious than that. So, don't turn your back on it!*

When we remember that the audience of Hebrews was facing a severe temptation to "recant" their belief in Jesus, or to somehow compromise their belief in Jesus as the true "emperor," then we see the point of this passage. The author is begging them to not be shortsighted and do something stupid.

It would have been very difficult for a Jew to abandon the "message spoken by angels" in order to follow a Galilean carpenter's son who claimed to be the Messiah. After all, the Law came from angels, the most incredible and god-like creatures imaginable, and Jesus was just some Joe, right? That would have been the Jewish argument against the claims of Jesus had He simply spoken words about the Kingdom of God. If the message was to be recognized as something from God that could supercede the angelic hosts, then it had to be accompanied by a great flurry of "super-angelic" signs and wonders. The power of the resurrection, the miracles performed by Jesus and the apostles, and the supernatural gifts given to followers of Jesus were the only calling card of God that would have spoken to the minds of the angel adoring Jews. The author reminds his readers that the Kingdom of God, their salvation, was just this kind of message. They should hold on to that truth and not let go.

HEBREWS

5-18 Yet, He Became Like Us in Order to Make His Message Work

There are three important lessons we can glean from this passage: regarding angels, regarding Jesus' death, and regarding temptation.

Regarding Angels

1. The angels are not the rulers of the Heavens. They do not lord it over humanity or sit in judgment over them. In fact, they have no power over them at all; good ones or bad ones. Jesus is the one who rules over the Heavens and the Earth, and He doesn't need angels to do it for Him.
2. The Kingdom of God isn't about angels. The Jews thought the angels were created to go back and forth between God and man and act as "emissaries," thus making it impossible for man to have direct relationship with God. The message of Hebrews tells the reader that this understanding of angels is all wrong. The good news of Jesus is that He bypassed the whole angelic system and came directly to humanity. Not only did He come to humanity, He became human in order to free humanity from the darkness that it experienced apart from their rightful place in relationship with God.
3. Jesus is not an angel, as some later Jewish rabbis taught. He is God who became human in order to reestablish humanity in its rightful place. Sorry, angels.

Regarding Jesus' Death

This passage speaks directly about the purpose of Jesus' death. The author quotes two Old Testament passages and from each he draws some beautiful parallels from which we can learn a great deal. The first passage is Psalm 22:22 and the second is Isaiah 8:17-18.

The Psalm 22 passage has two layers of meaning from which the author draws. The first layer is the Psalm itself. When you read the entire Psalm, you see that it is a Psalm of deep anguish and lament. The Psalmist is suffering greatly at the hands of his enemy. His suffering is so intense that he wonders if God has abandoned him. The Psalm can be paraphrased like this:

Faith that Transcends

> *God, why aren't you rescuing me? All of the people who hate you are surrounding me and they want to destroy me. I can barely endure this suffering. If you rescue me, I will proclaim your name to all the nations. I will make things as they should be. The poor will be helped and they will be equals with the rich. All nations will know who you are and I will be a blessing to everyone, for generations to come!*

The readers of Hebrews could definitely relate to the suffering of the Psalmist. As they were being tempted to abandon their faith they may have wondered if God had abandoned them. This however, was not the real point of the Psalm. Let's look at the second level to see the real impact. This Psalm was quoted by Jesus on the cross. In Matthew 27:46 he cried out, "My God, My God, why have you forsaken me?" It is most likely that Matthew recorded this, the first line of Psalm 22, to indicate that Jesus was both quoting the entire Psalm and also relating His experience of crucifixion with the message of the Psalm. That is where the Psalm, Jesus, and Hebrews intersect.

In verse 22 the Psalmist, and Jesus, in light of his deliverance from the enemy, exclaim,

> *I will declare your name to my brothers;*
> *in the congregation I will praise you.*
> *You who fear the LORD, praise him!*
> *All you descendants of Jacob, honor him!*
> *Revere him, all you descendants of Israel!*
> *For he has not despised or disdained*
> *the suffering of the afflicted one;*
> *he has not hidden his face from him*
> *but has listened to his cry for help.*

The point of this Psalm was to show that 1) Jesus was willing to suffer the pain of persecution in order to bring salvation to humanity, 2) God had not abandoned Jesus, but had used His suffering for the good of humanity, and 3) Jesus called us His brothers, making us part of God's family in order to restore us to our Heavenly Father.

Before we try to understand what Jesus' death is all about, let's look at the second Old Testament passage that was quoted and see what parallel we can draw from it. The quotes found in verse 13 come from Isaiah 8:17-18. If you took the time to go back to that passage in Isaiah, you would find that Isaiah was writing during a very volatile time in the history of the Northern Kingdom of Israel. The Israelites had been steeped in idol worship for generations and they were about to reap the fruit of their sin. The mighty Assyrian army was building up steam and were on the march toward Israel. They were hell-bent on destroying the Israelites. It was Isaiah's job to warn the Kingdom that destruction was coming. The Israelites would hear nothing of it. They mocked Isaiah and accused him of being overreactive to a mild situation that would soon blow over. God told Isaiah to hold his ground and not give in to the taunts and temptations of the Israelites. It is in this context that we find the words of Isaiah quoted here in Hebrews. As he stands his ground he says, "I will declare your name to my brothers; in the presence of the congregation I will sing your praises." Then, as the flood of Assyria's conquest crashes in on Israel, Isaiah huddles with his own children and says, "Here am I, and the children God has given me." In the earlier chapter his literal children had been born as a symbol of both the remnant that God would preserve through the conquests and the "child born of a virgin" who would be called "Immanuel, God with us."

The parallel continues as we read a little further in Isaiah. God had used a wicked nation like Assyria to bring punishment on His children. But, the Assyrians were proud and thought that they were the most powerful force in the universe. God had a message for the Assyrians. They, too, would be crushed because of their arrogance. God would wipe them out and, one day the Messiah would rule the earth. God would destroy the destroyer and once more establish His kingdom on Earth.

As we look at the rest of Hebrews chapter 2, with this Isaiah lens on, we can see a direct parallel. Humans are God's children, as were the Israelites. They strayed from God's ways and they needed punishment, just like the Kingdom of Israel did. So, God brought death to punish them, just like He brought the Assyrians to punish Israel. Here we must interject that the Jews associated death with Satan and many believed Satan to be the angel of Death. So, Satan/Death, stand in the place of Assyria in the analogy. Satan/Death arrogantly thinks it rules the universe. In response, God destroys the destroyer through the death of Jesus and establishes life once again for the world. Now Jesus, through His death, has brought the light of life to the "remnant," the "children of God" as He promised He would do to Isaiah so many years before. Now Jesus can say, along with Hosea and Paul,

> "Where, O death, is your victory?
> Where, O death, is your sting?

Faith that Transcends

Jesus death proved three things:

1. God loved humanity enough to suffer and die for it.
2. Jesus declared that humans are His brother, giving them rights as sons to come directly to God without fear or any angelic "in-betweens".
3. The fear of death has been destroyed. Think about that for a moment. We know that Jesus' followers still physically die, so how can death be conquered? What was conquered was the fear that is associated with death. Isn't fear the greatest tool of Satan to immobilize people? We shrink away from the things we fear and stay stagnant rather than adventure out in faith and obedience to God. Jesus' death conquered fear. Through Jesus we have confidence to know that God loves us, that we can come into His presence as children, and that death is simply a transfer, not the end. In light of this confidence we can live boldly in the Kingdom of God and be radically obedient to Jesus' commands to love everyone and be the conduit of His blessing to all people. That's pretty cool.

Regarding Temptation

At the end of the chapter the author introduces a new image that will be developed a great deal in chapters to come. He claims that Jesus is the great High Priest that made atonement for our sins. Since we'll cover that in detail later, we'll let that alone for the moment and look at one last point. The author claims that since Jesus was tempted, He is able to help those who are being tempted. What is he really saying here? How was Jesus tempted? There are two places where Jesus is tempted. The first was in the wilderness, just after His baptism. The second was just before His crucifixion. In both instances what was His temptation? Basically, He was tempted to take the easy road. He could have bypassed hunger by making His own bread from rocks. He could have called down angels to rescue Him and thus display His power. And, He could have simply established His rule over the earth by simply taking it and imposing it upon humanity. After all, He was the rightful ruler anyway. Then, in the last moments of His freedom, He contemplated having the cup removed from Him so that He would not have to suffer.

Yet, He resisted. He did not take the easy path. Why not? I believe Jesus had to suffer because He knew that the only way we would be saved is if we don't give into the temptation to take the easy road. This message was very pertinent to the Hebrew readers. They were facing the same temptation as Jesus. Should they give in and bypass persecution? No. Why not? Because it is only when we die to that kind of thinking and do what we know to be right that we can walk in the Kingdom of God. To sell out is to turn away from God's face and live in the darkness. Jesus came to give light and to demonstrate that His way is possible, even if it means death. Don't give up!

While we may not be faced with the intensity of the Hebrews' temptation, every day we are tempted to make small compromises and sell ourselves out to sin and self-destructive behavior. We aren't willing to go the extra mile with people to work out our differences. Instead we cut them off and intensify the isolation. When we see injustice we turn the other way because to intervene would be too much of an inconvenience. We succumb to some form of physical desire that counterfeits for intimacy or medicates loneliness because the work of human relationships is too difficult to bear. Whatever your temptation may be, we can find assurance that Jesus understands the struggle. As we will see throughout Hebrews, we can look to Him as our example and draw strength from Him to keep on keeping on.

Faith that Transcends

HEBREWS

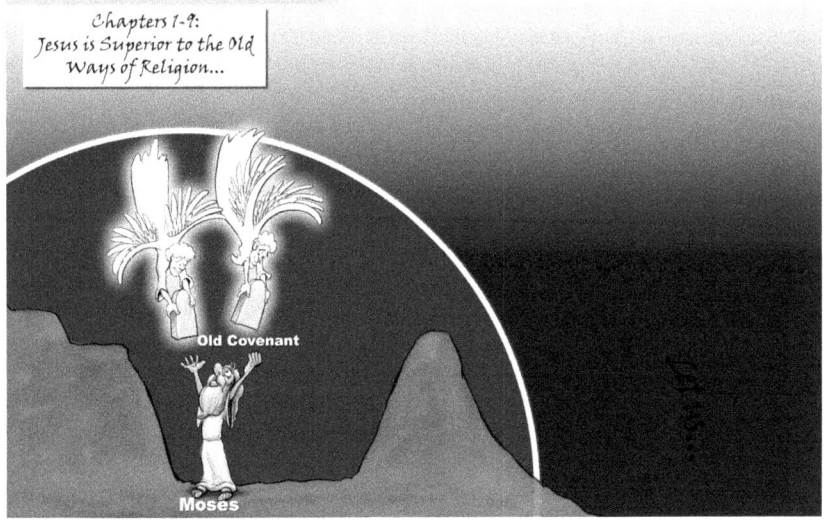

Lesson 3: Jesus is Greater than Moses

- Read: Hebrews 3

Study Questions

1. In what ways is Jesus compared and contrasted to Moses?

2. How are "we" described in verse 6? What condition is placed on this? Why?

3. Read Psalm 95. Rephrase this Psalm in your own words.

4. Meribah and Massah refer to a story from Exodus. Read Exodus 15:22-17:7 and see how many parallels and analogies you can find that may be applicable to the message that the author of Hebrews is trying to convey to his audience.

Food For Thought

In this section the author makes one simple point in verses 1-6 and then illustrates this point in verses 7-19 with an analogy from the Exodus.

A Son, not a Servant (1-6)

In chapters 1-2 the author argues from scripture that Jesus is superior to the angels. We discussed why this was a necessary first argument because the predominant Jewish theology of angels needed to be deconstructed in order to correctly understand the nature and role of Jesus as the only intermediary necessary between humans and God. Now, in chapter 3, we see another bastion of the faith deconstructed and put into proper perspective in the grand scheme of God's plan. The number one hero of the Jews was Moses. He was the great leader who delivered them from the tyranny of slavery in Egypt. He demonstrated God's power against the gods of Egypt and defeated the mightiest empire in the world. Moses was also the recipient of the Law. Moses climbed Mt. Sinai, into the very presence of God, and received God's specific instructions on how they should live. Ever since that day the Jews have considered those laws to be the definitive word on how God wants them to live forever and for always. They gauged their sense of "right" and "wrong" on these laws. They checked their own heart and determined their own sense of right standing with God based upon their adherence to these laws. If ever there was a human being that was as close to God as physically and spiritually possible, it was Moses. To question him would be heresy of the highest order.

In this passage the author of Hebrews brings perspective to the role of Moses in God's Kingdom. The image is very simple. God's house is not a tent or a building. Instead, God's house is His people. It always has been and it always will be. Moses was simply a servant in God's house. He was a hired hand contracted to lead the people like a shepherd leads sheep. This is a noble task and he did it very well. He deserves honor, but he was ultimately no different than any other human. Jesus is much more than that. Jesus built the house itself. He is our creator. The great miracle is that the creator of the house humbled himself to take on the role of the servant (just like Moses) in order to lead the people into a new and deeper understanding of what it actually means to be God's house – God's Kingdom – in the world.

Before we move to the next section, let's take a moment and look at verse 6. The original Greek language and structure of this sentence is fascinating and affords us a wonderful point of contemplation and application. Following the Greek syntax, the sentence literally reads like this:

Christ but as son over the house of him, whose house are we, if indeed the boldness and the bragging of the hope we hold on.

That's a little awkward in English. The NRSV gets the closest translation:

> *Christ, however, was faithful over God's house as a son, and we are his house if we hold firm the confidence and the pride that belong to hope.*

The two words that jump out at me in this passage are "confidence" and "pride." The Greek word for "confidence" means a person who has a big mouth and is bold enough to speak out in the public assembly. The Greek word for "pride" means to boast or to brag. Doesn't that seem a bit strange? Aren't Christians supposed to be humble and soft spoken? Isn't the Holy Spirit supposed to transform us and cleanse us from arrogance, pride, and self-exaltation? Yes, the Spirit does cleanse us from self-exaltation and arrogance that flows from a belief in self-importance and self-sufficiency. However, notice carefully where the boldness and bragging flows in verse 6. It flows from hope. When we believe that God loves us and that Jesus has invited us into life with God, both now and forever, then we are filled with courage and boldness. We are filled with the kind of pride that comes from realizing that we are associated with the purest and most wonderful thing in the entire universe. It is not the kind of boldness and pride that causes you to be an obnoxious jerk that says, "nerny, nerny, boo-boo, I'm a Christian and you're not." Of course not. It is the kind of boldness and pride that allows you to look down the muzzle of a gun and say, "if you shoot me, I will simply die, and God will still love you. I am not afraid because I am a child of God." Here is the point the author is trying to drive home to the Hebrews, and to us, as they stood, teetering on the edge of betrayal. Don't give up. Be confident, take bragging rights in the hope that God has given you through Jesus, the builder of the house!

HEBREWS

No Whiner-Babies! (7-19)

He met his Waterloo.

He crossed his Rubicon.

Do these phrases mean anything to you? If they don't then my analogy loses its initial punch, but I can still work with it. If you do know what they mean, then you'll nod your head along with this explanation as it serves to introduce and illustrate this section. Waterloo was where Napoleon came to the end of his rope and his attempt at world conquest was thwarted. The term "waterloo" has come to be a cultural phrase applied to anyone who fails. The Rubicon was the name of the river that Julius Caesar crossed in defiance of the law. By crossing this river with his troops he had committed himself to establish himself as the emperor of Rome. The term Rubicon is another cultural phrase that has come to mean, "passing the point of no return." These are examples of historical events that have taken on archetypal symbolism.

If you were a Jew in the first century and someone said to you, "Remember Meribah," you would wag your head in knowing despair. Meribah was the place just east of the Red Sea where the Israelites grumbled against God, quarreled against Him, and began their downward spiral in the wilderness. God had just delivered them from slavery in Egypt, miraculously defeated the greatest war machine in the world in the Red Sea, and had promised to take them across the desert so that they could move into the land he had promised to Abraham several generations earlier. Yet, in spite of all that goodness and power and grace, the people had the audacity to grumble and complain at the first sight of trouble. Eventually their bitterness, complaining, and resistance against God led them to be denied entrance into the Promised Land. They had to live out their days in the stark wilderness. For the Jew, that entire scenario was symbolized in the words "Meribah" and "Massah." Much like "Waterloo" and "Rubicon."

It is with this background in mind that we must read Hebrews 3:7-19. The author is simply saying, "Don't make that mistake again." He is drawing an analogy both for the first audience and for us. As believers, we have just been delivered from slavery to sin, just as the Israelites had been delivered from slavery to Egypt. Within two months of God's miraculous deliverance the people began to grumble and complain against God. When the water was bitter they complained, and God made the water sweet. When they had no food they complained and God provided miraculous bread every day for 40 years. When they were, again, thirsty, they complained and God caused water to come out of the rock. Eventually the grumbling and complaining cost the entire generation their inheritance of rest in the land promised to Abraham. Their entire attitude for the 40 years is symbolized by the bitter waters of Meribah. All God wanted to do for them was to provide them rest, and all they could do at the first sign of apparent discomfort was to complain and quarrel against God.

The author of Hebrews is making a strong analogy for his audience between their current situation of persecution and the trials faced by the Israelites. He says, "All God wants is for you to be delivered from sin and enter into the inheritance that is yours. Yes, the journey there may be riddled with war, hunger, thirst, and various difficulties, but don't give up. God will always provide for your every need, just like he provided manna. However, He will not tolerate quarreling with Him. If you turn your back on Him you will have no where to go except to yourself. You will wander out in the wilderness all by yourself, groping for the way back to Egypt, but finding only isolation and despair. If only you would grasp on to the truth that Jesus has paved the road to the inheritance for you. A few bumps in the road, a little persecution here and there, hey, maybe even your execution, is a small trial to endure when you consider the fact that you have the hope of being an heir to all the glory of the creator of the universe. Don't give up. Don't quarrel with God. Just believe that He has your best interest in mind, that He will provide your needs, and hold on to that courage and the bragging that comes from that kind of hope (v. 6)"

Even though we will probably not face persecution or death today, we may experience circumstances that will seem very difficult. What are the things that are weighing us down right now? What are the difficulties we are facing? Are there health issues that worry us? Do we have strains in our relationships? Whatever it may be, let us step back from it and see it in the perspective of the bigger picture of life. Let us remember that life and spiritual formation is a journey. Sometimes it will be easy, sometimes it will be difficult. Yet, through it all God is there, leading us and providing for us. The big issue in all of this is how we will respond to whatever circumstance comes up. Will we join the Israelites and whine about how good it was back in our slavery to sin and blame God for picking on us. Or, will we enter into an attitude of thankfulness as we realize that the difficult times will serve to strengthen us and prepare us for the larger journey that lies ahead. Let's listen to this chapter and not give up hope as we trust in the fact that God offers us His rest today and everyday if we will simply enter into it.

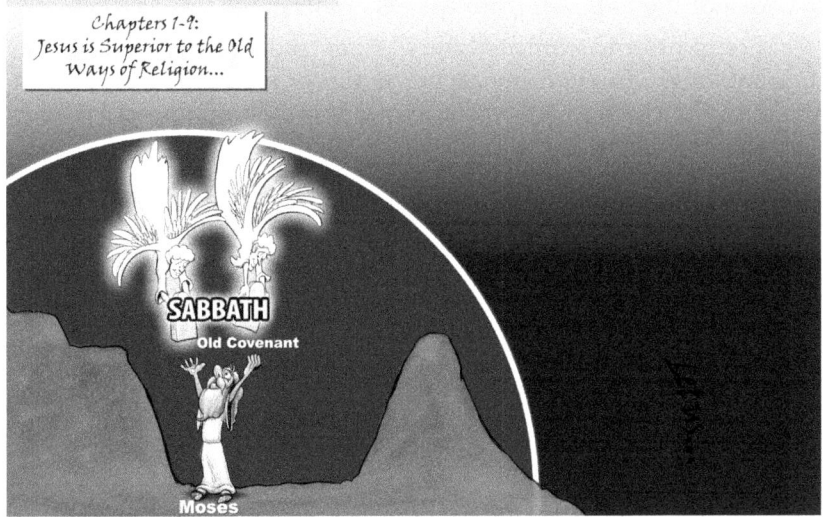

Lesson 4: The Deep Sabbath

- Read: Hebrews 4

Study Questions

1. What kept people from entering into the rest that God promised?

2. In order to understand this passage we must investigate the idea of the Sabbath from the Old Testament.

   Compare and contrast these three passages regarding the Sabbath. In each one, what is the purpose of the Sabbath and the example given for why it should happen, and who is the beneficiary?

   Exodus 20:8-11

   Deuteronomy 5:12-15

   Isaiah 56:1-8

3. Read the following passages and note what each type of Sabbath accomplishes.

   Leviticus 16:29-4

   Leviticus 25:1-7

HEBREWS

4. What was Jesus' perspective on the Sabbath in Mark 2:27-28? Why?

5. After reading these passages, try to explain the Sabbath in your own words.

6. When is the New Sabbath that God communicated to David?

7. Summarize verses 12-13 in your own words. How do these verses relate to the rest of chapter 4?

Food for Thought

It's pretty safe to say that much of our life is spent swimming in a chaotic sea of busy-ness. There is the constant white noise of activity buzzing around us. We drive on busy streets, we stand in crowded check-out lines, and we travel the well worn rut from home to work, punching in the clock. Even when we are not working we have activities that we rush to and music or television droning constantly in our ears. We run hard and fast.

Do you ever feel like you need a break? I was talking with a friend recently about a vacation to the beach that he took with his wife and three children. Several families camped on the beach and there were tons of kids running around. When he got home he was ready for a vacation from the vacation. Isn't it funny how we do that to ourselves all the time? We have this deep belief that we must be active all the time. But, when we are in the grind we want to take a break.

This chapter of Hebrews is all about taking a break and getting away from it all. In the language of Hebrews it is called Gods' rest. From the beginning of the story God has been inviting humanity into a place of rest with Him, and we have been slapping Him in the face for it. Ever since Adam first broke a sweat to till the soil and Eve had to grimace to give birth, life has been hard work for humans. We work and grind just to survive, and we don't like it. We dislike it so much that we are willing to conquer and subjugate others just to alleviate some of our own pain. The advent of sin has thrown us into this laborious grind called life. God looks at that and says, "No, that is not what you were created to be. I created you for LIFE, not life in the grind. Even though you brought this on yourself, I want to create a way for you to know freedom and peace. I want you to know what rest is really all about."

The word used throughout the Bible to represent this kind of rest that God has created for us and invited us into is "Sabbath." In this chapter the author exposes us to three kinds, or levels, of Sabbaths.

- The Sabbath of the Promised Land
- The Law of the Sabbath
- The Deep Sabbath

The Sabbath of the Promised Land

The opening verses of this chapter continue the theme from chapter 3 where we saw the Israelites out in the wilderness with Moses, grumbling about their difficult circumstances. As the story continues we see that the people eventually blew it completely. Even though God had clearly and directly given them the good news that they were going to occupy the Promised Land and experience rest from their oppression, they continued to doubt. They just could not believe that God could or would take them through the wilderness, against violent enemies, and into a place of settled peace. And so, they didn't get it.

Isn't that sad? That's like a man who is dying of thirst rejecting a glass of water. Why would he do it? Perhaps he doesn't trust the one offering the water. Perhaps he doesn't believe that water is actually the cure to thirst. So, the man stares at the glass of water as his throat dries shut and he dies. Was that the fault of the one extending the water? The author of Hebrews is simply warning his listeners to not make that mistake again. If they give in to the persecution they will be denying all the good that God is offering them in exchange for nothing but ultimate death.

The Law of the Sabbath

If you were a Jew during the time of Hebrews and you heard the word Sabbath it would connect to many deep emotions, ideas, and rituals. The Sabbath was a ritual that had been practiced in Israel since the time of Moses. From sundown on Friday night to sundown on Saturday night the Jews were not allowed to work. They weren't allowed to do anything except go to the synagogue for worship and spend a restful day at home eating food that had been prepared the day before.

Many of the Jews strictly obeyed this law because they believed it was directly tied to their current persecution. They were painfully aware that one of the many reasons the Israelites had been carried off into exile in generations prior was because they had abused the Sabbath. They did not let the people rest or let the land rest. The people in the first century wanted to be free from Roman oppression so they intensified the law of the Sabbath and scared everyone into observing it for fear of the wrath of God. They hoped that by their outward adherence to the law God would reward them with freedom from their oppressors.

The Deep Sabbath

The point of this chapter, in keeping with the themes of the previous chapters, is to demonstrate that Jesus has opened up for us a Sabbath Rest that is superior to the Sabbath of Moses and the expectations of the first century Jews. Jesus' rest is superior to and deeper than the physical inheritance of the Promised Land and the mechanical observance of not working on the seventh day of the week. The Good News of Jesus is that He came to reconnect us to the original intent for the Sabbath and call us into its deep, eternal reality.

Let's look at what the Sabbath was actually intended to accomplish in the lives of God's people. It was established to...

- rejuvenate the body/soil. Without physical rest on a regular basis our bodies will wear down and get sick. If the land doesn't lay fallow periodically it will be stripped of its nutrients and not produce healthy food, which will, in turn, lead to our demise.
- allow us to acknowledge trust that God is the provider, not our work.
- create equality within society; no one serves another on the Sabbath
- create space for us to focus our attention on relationship with God as Lord, Father, and Lover
- invite us into the rest that comes from knowing that we are at peace with God and that, because of God's Grace, we can join him at the table and eat with Him.

The Sabbath truly was, as Jesus said, created for man by a loving God. Just like good parents create bedtimes and make children eat their vegetables, so does God establish the Sabbath. The problem comes down to whether we believe it is for our own good or not. Belief is the same word as faith. The problem with the Israelites in the wilderness was that they didn't have faith; they didn't believe God. The problem with the legalistic Jews was that they didn't have faith in God; they had faith in their own efforts. Ironically they were "working" to not work on the Sabbath. Jesus calls us to have faith; to trust that God's Word is true. God loves you, He has made peace with you through Jesus, and He provides for you. Do you believe it?

HEBREWS

When you break the Sabbath you demonstrate lack of faith and cut yourself off from the rest that God offers. This happens in many ways. When you break the deep Sabbath...

- You wear down your body by overworking it, thereby weakening your immune system and opening yourself up for sickness. You are probably also shortening your lifespan by not getting proper rest.

- You are saying, "No, I HAVE to work because if I don't then I will not survive. I don't believe that God will provide my needs. It's all up to me."

- You are not creating space for people to leave their artificially constructed socio-economic roles and enter into a family of equality atmosphere where the rule of the day is relaxed fellowship. In so doing you are perpetuating a pampered-stay-pampered and the-oppressed-stay-oppressed scenario in society. This is contrary to the Kingdom of God.

- You are perpetuating a distracted lifestyle in which you never take time to slow down and examine your heart. God is a patient and quiet lover who will wait silently on the couch, watching you toil away, wishing you would simply sit and talk with Him for a while.

- You, whether in actions or words, communicate to God, "I don't believe you truly love me. I don't believe you have made peace with me. Either I am afraid of you, thinking that you might pull a fast one on me, or I am afraid to expose myself to you because I believe that you couldn't possibly love me with all the shameful things I think, say, and do. No, God, I'd rather stay out here on my own where I don't have to be vulnerable to you or anyone else. I'll just eat my meal alone, thank you."

The great thing about the deep Sabbath is that it is not an external ritual or law that can become an oppressive system. It is a matter of the heart. That is what verses 12-13 are all about. Many people struggle with how these verses relate to the rest of the chapter. At first read they don't seem to flow. Part of the reason they don't seem to flow is because these verses are most familiar to us after they have been ripped out of context and used to refer to the Bible. In context, however, I believe these verses go much deeper than that. The Word of God is so much more than the ink on paper that we call the Bible. Yes, the Bible contains the inspired and authoritative record of the Word of God, but the Word of God is the powerful interaction that God has with us directly. David had the Word of God as He was intimate with God. It was to David that God revealed the Deep Sabbath and liberated us from the letter of the Law. You see, the Word of God doesn't care about external behavior. The Word of God looks at your heart. It -- He -- cuts through all the smoke screens and facades that we construct that are designed to fool other people, and He gets right to the Deep reality of who we are. It is here that God invites us into the Deep Sabbath Rest that Jesus has provided.

The great thing about the deep Sabbath is that it is not bound up in time and space. It is Today. It is right now. It does not matter if you have blown it yesterday, because it is Today. God's grace is real. Jesus' work is done. He is at rest. He sits in a state of Sabbath, being at peace with us, and He invites us in to eat with Him. Today. Right now. It is as easy as saying, "Thank You" and entering in.

HEBREWS

Lesson 5: Jesus is a Better High Priest

- Read: Hebrews 4:14-5:10

Study Questions

1. What are the two commands (or instructions) given in 4:14-16?

2. What will result from following these instructions? Why?

3. Read Leviticus 16. How were the Jews supposed to approach the Ark of the Covenant (the Throne of Grace)? Why?

4. How does this relate to Hebrews 4:16?

5. How is the high priest described?

6. What ways does Jesus fit the description of the High Priest?

7. In what ways does Jesus' ministry as a High Priest supercede that of the other High Priests?

8. What implications does that have for our lives?

HEBREWS

Food For Thought

You've heard of Chicken Soup for the Soul? Hebrews is Tossed Salad for the Spirit. That's right. Take a look through the whole book and you'll find that whenever the author calls his readers to action he pulls out the lettuce and tosses it up; let us do this...let us do that. (OK, so it's corny, but I bet you'll remember it). In this section we start off with two pieces of "let us". First he says, "let us hold fast our confession (NASB translation)" and secondly, he says, "Let us then approach the throne of grace with confidence."

Put in our language, the first "let us" says, "walk the talk." The word "confession" is the Greek word "homologia" which means "the same word, or agreement." Perhaps you have heard of churches or denominations talk about their "confession of faith." When you proclaim a homologia you are stating what you believe to be true; what you agree with. In the context of the readers of Hebrews, they were being asked to put their lives on the line for what they claim to believe. As followers of Jesus they had boldly proclaimed that Jesus is the supreme Lord of the entire universe. This was a direct attack on the supremacy of Caesar. Now the Romans were pressuring them to take back their confession or die. The author urges them to "krateo" their confession. This is a violent word that means to seize; to grab onto. He does not want them to say, "Yeah, I have a category in my mind that allows for Jesus to be Lord in concept." No, he says, "Grab onto that belief with all your might and cling to it, because it stands between you and death. Don't let go of it; it is everything."

The second "let us" reminds me of the Indian Jones movie Raiders of the Lost Ark. In that movie the Nazis are searching for the Ark of the Covenant which has been missing since the destruction of Jerusalem. In the final scene the Nazi army opens the Ark and looks inside. When they do an awesome power pours out of the ark and incinerates everyone around it. Poof! Up in smoke. The only ones who survive are Indy and the girl, because they respected the Ark and did not look at it.

Granted, that is Fantasy Adventure Filmmaking with cool special effects, however, it does tap into a very important reality. The Ark of the Covenant was something to be feared and respected by the Jewish people. It was not to be trifled with. The Ark was the physical representation of God's presence on Earth. On top of the Ark there were two, six-winged cherubim who pointed their wings to the center of the lid. This space between their wings was called the Mercy Seat or the Throne of Grace. In Leviticus 16 we read specific instructions to Aaron, the High Priest, that no one was to approach the Ark except the High Priest. Even then, the High Priest could only approach on one day a year and he had to go through a series of rituals before he could enter behind the curtain and into the presence of the Throne of Grace. If he did not follow these instructions carefully he would die.

The Old Testament is full of stories about the power of the ark and about people who were killed because they treated the ark with flippancy or indifference. It is in light of this collective community consciousness concerning the "Throne of Grace" that we must read Hebrews 4:16. "Let us approach the Throne of Grace with confidence." What?!? Are you crazy? Have you not read the Old Testament? We can't go before the throne of Grace. We need a High Priest to do it for us.

Now we see the significance of this passage. The Good News of Jesus presents two incredibly radical ideas to the Jewish people:

1. Jesus is the High Priest to end all High Priests. You no longer need a man like you to go through all the cleansing ceremonies to prepare himself to make atonement for the sins of the nation. Jesus has gone through the cleansing ceremony of humiliation, death, and resurrection, so that He can enter into the presence of the Throne of Grace once and for all time.

2. Because Jesus is the High Priest, you now have access to the Throne of Grace yourself. There is no longer a dividing curtain between you and God. The curtain has been torn wide open and the welcome mat has been laid out for you to come into God's presence and draw the strength and confidence you need to stand strong in the times of trial. Don't be afraid of the throne of Caesar. Yes, it may look big and intimidating as that self-exalted human parades himself throughout the Empire, demanding worship from his fellow creatures. Just remember that you have access to THE throne of the universe. Raise your eyes to the Heavens, above the head of that imposter, and draw strength from the ultimate reality of Jesus, the King and High Priest, that has served you and has set you free from the tyranny of this Earthly power structure and fear-based system.

HEBREWS

Throughout the upcoming chapters of Hebrews the author will expand on the idea of Jesus' ministry as the High Priest and the notion of him being a priest in the order of Melchizedek. We will save those concepts for later. For now, let's focus on the salad issues. Let us hold firmly our confession and approach the Throne with confidence. While the explanation of the priest and the Ark may have been interesting to you, perhaps it left you wondering, "What does this have to do with me?" That's a fair question. As Americans, we have no collective consciousness of the Almighty Throne of Grace being an impenetrable fortress of holiness before which we should bow in fear and trepidation. We have no concept of a humanly held position like the High Priest that represents our entire nation before God. To say that Jesus fills these positions, deconstructs them, and reconstructs them in a deeper, richer way does not have the oomph that it probably did for the 1st century Jewish believers.

So what do we do? First, we must realize that we probably have just the opposite problem. Our collective conscience is so used to the idea of an open throne room that we have probably tracked too much mud across the welcome mat as we scamper in and out, playing around at the foot of the Throne of Grace, forgetting that it still represents the same thing that it did when it was created. We are not invited into Grandpas sitting room to get our weekly lollipop and hear a neat story about the good ol' days. We are given a special privilege to come before the presence of the Almighty creator of the universe; the very power of life itself. This is a privilege and an honor. Let us not forget that and let us treat it – and Him – with the honor due His Name.

Secondly, we need to remember that there are still Caesars parading around our world, demanding allegiance and worship. They may be literal political systems that demand allegiance. Or, more subtly, they may be ideologies that lure us into believing that we are autonomous individuals that do not need anyone's help to survive in life. We don't need a God to save us. We don't need a High Priest to represent us. We don't need a community to protect us, admonish us, and empower us. We can do it on our own. Perhaps the greatest Caesar that demands our allegiance is the illusion of our Autonomous Self.

As we ponder this thought, let's look at the model of Jesus. The one person who had the right to demand worship from all humans is the one person who emptied Himself of that right and became humbled. He became human. He was tempted. He suffered. He became dependent upon the power of God to help Him through the trials of human life – and human execution – in order to become perfect. He did this for us. He did this to show us that unless we die to the idea that we are self-sufficient units in the universe, we will die. We must humble ourselves and realize that we need God, that we need each other, and that we must become purified through the trials of life. As we look to Jesus, our High Priest, we can draw upon His example of humility and reliance upon God to show us how we can stand strong during our experiences of difficulty in life.

HEBREWS

Lesson 6: Grow Up and Hang On!

- Read: Hebrews 5:11-6:20

Study Questions

1. Why does the author say his teaching is hard to understand?

2. How are the mature described?

Faith that Transcends

3. What are the elementary teachings?

4. State the author's warning found in 6:4-8 in your own words.

5. What is the author's opinion of his reader's stamina? Upon what does he base this opinion?

6. Upon what did God stake his promise to Abraham?

7. What analogy is used to describe the promise that God has made? Why?

HEBREWS

Food for Thought

If our last lesson was a tossed salad full of "let us" then this section is a Melchizedek sandwich. In 5:10 the author says, "[Jesus] was designated by God to be a high priest in the order of Melchizedek." If you skip over our current section and continue reading in 7:1 it reads, "This Melchizedek was a king of Salem and priest of God Most High...." What is said between 5:10 and 7:1 is a parenthetical note that was sparked by the mention of Melchizedek; a Melchy sandwich.

Let me attempt a loose paraphrase to get at what is going on behind this section:

> *Jesus is not just your run-of-the-mill high priest. In fact, He is such an extraordinary High Priest that He breaks all the rules of the high priest. What I'm about to tell you regarding Melchizedek and Jesus' relation to him may sound far fetched and hard to grasp. That's because you are still little children. You are still stuck on the ABC's of the Good News about Jesus and aren't ready to handle this deep truth.*

> *Be careful. If you don't grasp this deep truth then you might be tempted to succumb to the pressures that surround you and denounce Jesus just to save your skin. If you do that, then the future does not look bright for you. It is next to, if not completely, impossible to pull yourself out of a hole like that.*

> *But don't worry. I believe that you are made of stronger stuff than that. I think you will understand what I am about to tell you regarding Melchizedek and that you will grasp hold of it. When you do, you will realize that it is the very thing you needed to stand strong during these troubled times.*

> *Why is it so important to grasp this? It is important because it touches on the one key principle of God's Kingdom: PROMISE. God has promised that He will be faithful to His people and that He will make things right. It is our faith, our steady belief, in this promise that will carry us through the storms of these trials. When you follow Abraham's example and have faith, then it will become like an anchor for your soul. When trials, temptations, and difficult times blow through your life you will be able to reach into the Holy Place,*

the very heart of God, and know that He loves you and has your best interest in mind. If you do not believe this, then you will be blown away by the difficulties and you will be lost. You will be like the barren land that produces no useful crops. All you have will simply be burned up and vanish.

Don't give up hope. Believe in God's Promise. Got the picture? Now, let's get on with this business about Melchizedek.

The ABC's of the Good News (5:11-6:6)

In this section the author gets pretty harsh with his readers. He basically calls them spiritual babies and tells them to grow up. They are addicted to the baby bottle and aren't ready for solid food. It may be very easy for us to blow past this section and think that we understand it. "Yeah, yeah, we should be digging deeper into 'meatier' stuff, like doctrine and theology or studying the original languages of the text. So I'm a baby, I can't help it." Let's spend a little time and look closer at this section. You may be surprised at what the author considers "milk" and what is "meat."

In 5:12 the Greek reads like this, "again you have the need to be taught the basic elements (stoicheia) of the beginning of the words of God..." The word "stoicheia" is only used 7 times in the New Testament. Paul uses it 4 times; twice in Galatians 4 and twice in Colossians 2. In the Greek culture if you were to say "stoicheia" most people would immediately think about the basic elements that Plato taught -- earth, air, fire, water. These are the basic building blocks upon which everything else is built. In Paul's letters to the Galatians and Colossians he considers the Law of Moses to be a "stoicheia" and warns the people to not turn back to these "basic elements" or else they will enslave them and rob them of the power and beauty of Jesus' Kingdom. Here, in Hebrews, we see another warning against being stuck in the "stoicheia" and, thus being weakened by them. Instead, we should be sinking our grown-up teeth into the solid food.

HEBREWS

So, what is the milk? In 6:1-2 he lists the "stoicheia":
- repentance from dead works
- faith in God
- teaching about ceremonial washings (baptisms)
- laying on of hands
- resurrection of the dead
- eternal judgment

At this point you may be thinking, "Wait a minute! That sounds like an outline for a course in Theology at a Bible School or seminary. How could that be milk?" There is an important point that we should understand about this list. It is not an exclusively Christian list of belief topics. Any good Jew in the 1st century would have agreed that these were essential topics. Think back to our studies of Jesus' conversations with the teachers of the Law and the controversies that Peter and Paul had with them in the book of Acts. The controversies were over these issues. The Pharisees and the Sadducees were constantly going at it over the issue of the resurrection of the dead and the state of eternity. They were always bickering about the observance of ceremonial washings and the proper level of repentance to demonstrate the right amount of faith in God. Jesus shut them down by deconstructing their arguments and telling them they were asking the wrong questions. Peter and Paul bypassed judgment by dividing the Sanhedrin over these issues.

Let's look at the church of today. What do we tend to do? We like to construct elaborate doctrinal "confessions" about the exact and proper way to believe and articulate each of these points. Then we launch grenades at our brothers who do not agree with us. In the process we divide the church and lose our focus on the whole purpose of Jesus' mission in the world. Look what the author says back in 5:14, "Solid food is for the mature, who by constant use have trained themselves to distinguish good from evil." The words good and evil are "kalos" and "kakos." They can be rendered "useful for the purpose" and "unuseful, or contrary to the purpose." A person who has tapped into the deep mystery of Jesus, and has trained himself to follow the ways of Jesus and trust in the love of God, realizes that all the bickering over the "stoicheia" is "unuseful, or contrary to the purpose" of Jesus' mission to bring restoration and peace to the world.

As it was with the Jews, so it is with the church today. We spend our time sloshing around in the baby pool of "doctrinal distinctives" that our various sects have constructed and miss out on the ocean expedition into the mystery of following the Living Lord Jesus into uncharted territories of life.

A Warning (6:4-12)

The author continues to drive the point home by saying, "if you continue to bicker about these things you will produce nothing but thorns and thistles. Your soul will be dry, and when the day of testing comes you will have nothing to grab hold of." Our faith is not built on our ability to correctly articulate the minute details of our doctrinal statements and have rational explanations for every question. Our faith comes from having a dynamic and living relationship with God, because of Jesus. When the Spirit of God lives in us it produces fruit in us. The fruit is the reflection of God's nature. It is real. Jesus told us that you will know a tree, not by what the tree says about itself, or about fruit, but by the actual fruit that the tree produces. It's that simple.

Remember, the overarching issue in this letter is the persecution the readers were facing at the hands of the Romans. The author is warning them to not make a stupid decision. He's telling them that renouncing Jesus to the Romans would be like selling your soul. Once it's sold, you can't get it back. You're done. So, don't do it.

Then he changes gears quickly and assures them that he believes they won't do it. He knows their hearts are good and that God's mercy is even deeper than they can imagine.

An Anchor for the Soul 6:13-20)

Have you ever seen the Disney movie Aladdin? In the opening scenes Aladdin is leading Jasmine through the streets of Agrabah as they are being chased by the royal guards. At one point they seem to be cornered with no way out. Aladdin reaches down and extends his hand to Jasmine and asks, "Do you trust me?" At that point Jasmine had to make a choice. Aladdin was going to do something that seemed counterintuitive and might get them killed. If she took his hand she would have to believe with all her

HEBREWS

heart that he could lead her to safety. In this section of Hebrews God, through Jesus, reaches out his hand to Abraham, and to us, and says, "Do you trust me?"

It all comes down to trust. The words "faith," "believe", and "trust" are all the same word in Greek: "pisteuo." We must pisteuo God. We must have faith. God has made a promise. He promised that He would make a great nation through Abraham and that through that nation the entire world would be blessed. He made a promise through Jesus that our sins would be forgiven and that we would be restored into a right relationship with God so that we, too, can participate in God's redemptive plan for creation.

He reaches out his hand and says "do you trust me?" Even when the Egyptian army is on your heals and the Red Sea lies in front of you, do you trust me? Even when there are giants in the land and the cards are stacked against you, do you trust me? Even when there is pain and suffering all around you, do you trust me? Even when the plans you thought I had for you don't seem to be working out, do you trust me? Even if you lose all the earthly things that seem to be a "blessing," do you trust me? Do you believe that I love you and have your best interest in mind? Do you trust that, regardless of your circumstances, you will be saved and know peace forever? If you do, then I will be an anchor for you when the painful trials of life threaten to blow you away. But, if you don't trust me, then you are on your own. My hand will always be extended. Do you trust me?

What areas are you struggling with today that make it hard for you to believe that God loves you? What circumstances seem to communicate a different message? Take a second look. Perhaps God is still there, working a plan for you that is deeper and richer than you could have imagined, but is not yet clear to see. Take his hand. He loves you.

Faith that Transcends

HEBREWS

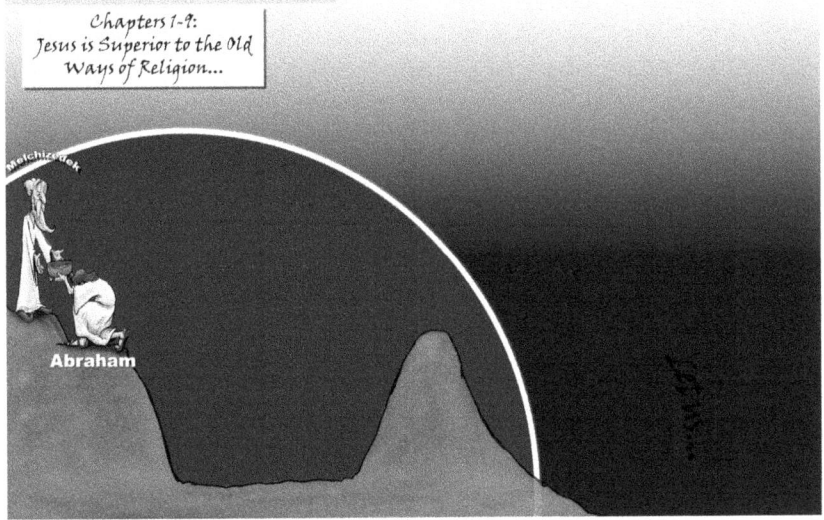

Lesson 7: Jesus is a Priest Like Melchizedek

- Read: Hebrews 7

Study Questions

1. Read Genesis 14:18-21. Observe the facts about Melchizedek. Who is he? What does he do? Why might this be important?

2. Read Psalm 110. To whom is David referring? What claims are made about this person?

3. Read Acts 2:29-36. How does Peter use Psalm 110 to explain the nature of Jesus?

4. Read Mark 12:35-40. How does Jesus use Psalm 110 to describe himself?

5. Compare the description of Melchizedek in Hebrews 7 with the account in Genesis 14. Where is it the same, where is it different? How might you account for the differences?

6. What is the relationship between Levi and Melchizedek? Why is this emphasized?

7. According to this passage, why is it important that Jesus be a priest in the order of Melchizedek?

HEBREWS

Food for Thought

A Peculiar Mystery

The Subject of Melchizedek has sparked the imagination of people throughout the ages. There is one simple reason why this character is so mysterious: we don't know much about him at all. His story occupies three or four verses in Genesis...that's it. He is an anomaly. Here, in the middle of pagan, idol-worshipping Canaan, appears a priest that Abram bows before. Where did that come from? The fact that he is an enigma has given huge liberty to people to "read between the lines" and create elaborate explanations for who he was, why he was significant, and why the author of Hebrews uses him as a credential for Jesus' role as High Priest.

Before we dive into this murky water, let's keep our focus on the big picture of Hebrews. The author is encouraging the Jewish Christians to stand strong in the face of severe persecution. He is building a case for the legitimacy of Jesus that will be a strong foundation to stand on and an anchor for the soul during the times of testing. One of the anchor points for his argument is the fact that Jesus is a Priest in the order of Melchizedek. When we read this piece of the argument we cock our head to the side like a confused puppy and say, "huh?" It just doesn't connect. We have to believe that his logic would have made sense to the 1st century reader, otherwise why would the author use it? He's not trying to confuse his people with obscure, esoteric theology; he's trying to encourage them with something solid in the face of real danger. So, the question for us is to figure out how the original hearers would have understood the phrase "in the order of Melchizedek."

Simply put, we can paraphrase chapter 7 like this:

> *Jesus is a priest like Melchizedek, not like Aaron. Melchizedek was a priest long before Aaron, or the Law of Moses, or even before the calling of Abram. In fact, Levi, Aaron's ancestor and the father of the priestly tribe, paid homage to Melchizedek when Abram paid him a tenth. Jesus is both a King and a Priest. His sacrifice is perfect and eternal. You do not have to worry. Jesus paid for your sin, has made peace with God for you, and he will not let you down.*

A Deeper Look

Now, for you who are curious about this Melchizedek person, let's dive in. Actually, we don't have the time or space to truly dive into these murky waters, so let's put on our snorkel mask and peek into it for a moment.

Let's begin our investigation with the simple facts from the four verses in Genesis 14:18-21

The simple facts:

- His name was Melchizedek.
- He was a King of Salem.
- He was the Priest of el elyon (Most High God)
- He brought bread and wine to Abram.
- He blessed Abram.
- Abram paid him a tenth of the spoils of war.

OK, that's it. That's all the hard evidence we have. Now, we must ask, "What do these facts mean? Is it possible to know for sure?" Let's look at each of the simple facts and discuss some of the various interpretations:

- Melchizedek. The name Melchizedek literally means "King of Justice," or "my King is justice," or "King of Zedek". One of the Canaanite gods was named Zedek (Justice).
- He was the King of Salem. Most scholars agree that this Salem was the same city that came to be known as Jeru-salem. It was later conquered by David and established as the capital city of Israel and the home of Solomon's temple to Jehovah. The Jews point to this as justification for the superiority of Jerusalem as God's holy city throughout all time. The word Salem means peace. Perhaps Salem was the one peaceful place in the middle of the warring factions of the Canaanite city-states; a picture of God's Kingdom on earth.
- He was the Priest of El Elyon (God Most High). Some scholars debate whether this name refers to Jehovah (Yahweh), the God of Abraham, or if it refers to a Canaanite God. During this period each city-state in Canaan worshipped its own ruling deity. The term el or al was present in all the names i.e. Ba-al. To say "el elyon" was simply to say the highest of the gods. However, in v. 22 we see that Abram combines these two names as he describes "the LORD (Yahweh), God Most

HEBREWS

High (el elyon), Creator of heaven and earth..." It is safe to say that Melchizedek served as priest to the God of the Bible, Jehovah. The real mystery is how and why this is possible? If God had an authentic priest serving him in Salem, why did he need to call Abram out of Ur and send him to Canaan? This issue is the one that has sparked so many different theories about the nature of Melchizedek's priesthood and his relationship to God. These theories range to far extremes. 1) The Jews, in the centuries prior to Jesus' life, theorized that Melchizedek was actually Shem, one of Noah's sons. He was the last surviving person that lived in the pre-flood era. At his meeting with Abram, Shem passed on the stories of creation and the fall to Abram to preserve within the nation of Israel. 2) Other Jews taught that at this meeting Abram received the law and passed it down through the generations. 3) Some Christians believe that Melchizedek was one of many appearances of Jesus in the Old Testament. This is called a Christophany. 4) On the other extreme end of the spectrum there are teachers from the Gnostic perspective that believe Melchizedek is actually Satan, the demiurge god that created the earth (or at least the priest to Satan) and that Jesus is in line with Satan (radical, but people teach it). In between these two extremes are all kinds of cults and metaphysical philosophies that claim Melchizedek as their founder. It seems that any time you want to start a new tradition you simply need to play the Melchizedek card to trump any objections.

- ◇ He brought bread and wine to Abram. As with the previous issue of his priesthood, many have attempted to interpret the significance of the bread and the wine. It could have been as simple as the fact that Melchizedek was offering hospitality to Abram and his men by serving them the basic staples of life: bread and wine. Of course, through Christian lenses it is difficult to not automatically see a typology for the bread and wine of the Eucharist present in this account. Most likely, this simple meal represents a covenant of peace and fellowship between Abram and Melchizedek. This is the space in which God desires to dwell with his people, and all who bless Abram will be invited to do so. It is to this table that Jesus invites us to eat with Him.

- ◇ He blessed Abram. When God made his initial covenant with Abram in Genesis 12, He said that anyone who blesses Abram will be blessed and anyone who curses Abram will be cursed. (Gen. 12:3) Here we see a clear example of that promise.

The King of Sodom did not bless Abram, but tried to barter with him. We know what happened to the city of Sodom. Melchizedek, on the other hand, blessed Abram, blessed God, and shared a common table with him. This is the true spirit of the way of God.

- ◇ Abram gave him a tenth. Once again, there are different theories as to why Abram would feel compelled to pay the King of Salem a tenth of his spoils. Typically, the payment of this type of tax or offering was deference to superiority. Abram was acknowledging that somehow Melchizedek was his superior. He was also acknowledging the covenant of peace (Salem) that Abram had entered.

So, what's the deal in Hebrews 7?

The readers of Hebrews were Jews that took great stock in the Old Testament Scriptures. One of the key passages from which Hebrews is based is Psalm 110. This Psalm was written by David and was probably composed in response to his defeat of the city of Salem (see 2 Samuel 5:6-16). Psalm 110 has already been quoted frequently throughout Hebrews. Some scholars believe that the entire letter to the Hebrews is actually an exposition of this Psalm. For us to understand all of Hebrews, and specifically this passage on Melchizedek we must understand how the 1st century Jews interpreted this Psalm. It is from this interpretation that the author of Hebrews builds his case for the priesthood of Jesus.

Let's look at Psalm 110 for a moment. It begins "the LORD (Yahweh) says to my lord (adoni)". The first question is who is talking to whom? Is God talking to David and encouraging him that he will rule from now on in Jerusalem and will be victorious over his enemies (which happened)? Or, is David prophesying about a future king that will come from his line that will rule from Jerusalem. This future king will not only be a King, but he will also be a Priest, just like Melchizedek was a priest and a king.

We know that the Jews must have put great stock in this passage because it plays a significant role in another message spoken in the New Testament. In Acts 2 Peter refers to this Psalm as he speaks to the crowd at Pentecost. He reminds them that David predicted this day would come when one of his offspring would sit on his throne eternally. Peter, in Acts 2:36, after quoting Psalm 110:1, said, "Therefore let all Israel be assured of this: God has made this Jesus, whom you crucified, both Lord and Christ." In the same vein, we also see Jesus use this passage in Mark 12:35-40. Obviously, the Jews put great stock in this passage, yet it remained enigmatic to them as well.

Psalm 110 was one of those passages that had woven its way into the collective psyche of the nation, so the name Melchizedek was always present, be it ever so cryptically, in the talk of the coming Messiah. Yet, in the context of the Psalm itself, it is fair to ask why David would even make the allusion to Melchizedek. If David had just defeated Jerusalem, the great story of Abram paying homage to the King of that city would be fresh on his mind. Here, from this ancient city, God would forever rule over his Kingdom of Peace, just like Melchizedek did.

We do not know exactly how the Jews interpreted this Psalm. Actually, there were various interpretations. The one thing they did know, and all agreed on, however, was that this Psalm was prophetic in nature and was pointing to a coming day when the Messiah would come and rule both as a King and a Priest, just like Melchizedek did. I believe that is the key to understanding Hebrews. According to Jewish law, there could never be a Priest/King. The Kings came from David, who was from the tribe of Judah. The Priests came from the tribe of Levi. A Judahite could never be a priest and a Levite could never be a king. Yet, the Messiah would be a King, a Priest, and a Prophet. The only way for this to happen would be to supercede the tribal laws and harken back to a more primal order of worship and relationship to God. The Kingdom of Peace (Salem) would once again be ruled by a Priest/King who would serve bread and wine to the nations and would bless God's people. This is Jesus.

What about us?

We don't talk much about priests and kings today. It would be easy to dismiss this lesson as irrelevant to our pluralistic, globalized world. However, perhaps now more than ever, we desperately need the ministry of the King/Priest. We need a leader who rules over us in peace, who leads us in worship of God, and who extends to us a meal of sustenance and fellowship. We need a leader who brings unity to the warring factions in the world; a healing between political leaders and spiritual leaders. We need Jesus. He is the leader who will guide us away from schisms and factions and will welcome us all into the Kingdom of Peace in the worship of God at his table.

Faith that Transcends

This week, as you travel through the chaos of modern life, imagine the King of Salem coming out to meet you. In his hand he holds nourishment and refreshment. He invites you to stop, sit down, reflect, and worship el elyon, the God Most High. He compels you to give your tenth and recalibrate your focus and desires. Only then will you regain your bearings and be filled with courage and strength to extend the Kingdom of Peace to the world around you.

HEBREWS

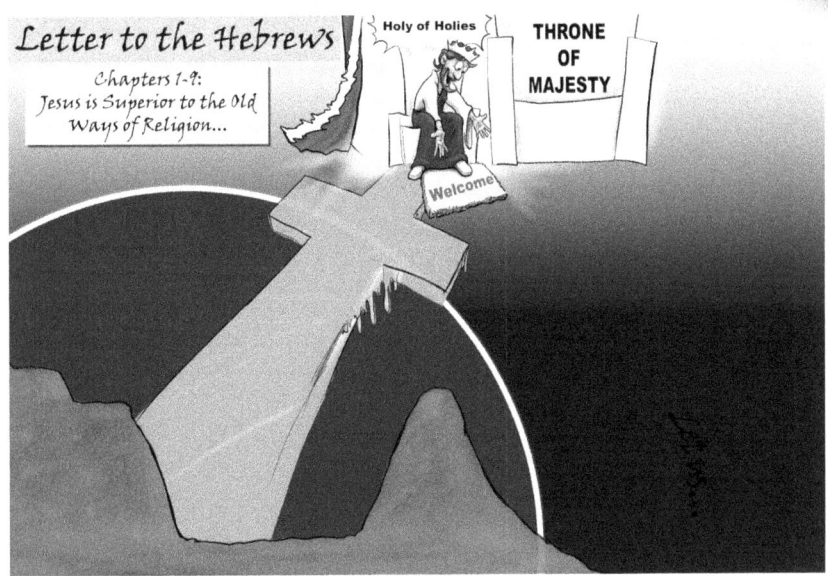

Lesson 8: A New Tent and Promise

- Read: Hebrews 8

Study Questions

Read Exodus Exodus 25:8-9;39:32-43;40:34-38.

1. What was the purpose of the tabernacle?

2. What is the correlation between the "true tabernacle" of Hebrews and the tabernacle found in Exodus?

Read Exodus 24 and 34.

3. In what way is the "new covenant" in Hebrews 8 different from the "old covenant" of Exodus?

HEBREWS

Food for Thought

The Point

The author gives us a beautiful gift in verse one. He tells us what his point is in writing these things. Here's a little Bible Study tip: whenever the author says, "here's my point," take notes, star it, underline it. Everything else around it either points to it or flows from it. The Greek word being translated is "Kephalaion" which comes from the root "kephalos" meaning "head." In a sense, this is the beginning of the climax of the letter, the place where it all comes to a head. Everything up to this point has been laying a foundation upon which this capstone can be supported. It would do us well to stop and take a moment to recap where we have been and see the argument from the bird's eye view:

Jesus is higher than the angels,
> yet He became lower than them, like us, to set us free.

Jesus is higher than Moses,
> so don't rebel like they did.

Jesus offers a superior Sabbath Rest to His people,
> so enter into it TODAY.

Jesus is higher than the Levitical High Priests (He's in the order of Melchizedek)

> SO.....here's the point:
> JESUS IS AN ETERNAL HIGH PRIEST THAT YOU CAN TRUST!

At this point we enter into a new section of the letter. In chapters 8-10 the author explains what it means for Jesus to be that kind of high priest. As we work through these three chapters we will discover that there seems to be a lot of repetition. For our minds this may seem like redundancy and become somewhat tedious, monotonous, and/or annoying. Before we tune out on this message we must remember that the author is using a common method of communicating in his day. In a preliterate society it was necessary to emphasize important points in a spoken message by repeating them throughout the message in slightly different ways. Each time he repeats a topic he delves a little deeper into its explanation. This was both a poetic form and also a mnemonic device that drove the point home to the listener. In other words, if you repeat it, the people will remember it. Rather than be annoyed, let's allow ourselves to use these chapters to soak into the topics and absorb as much as we can from their intended meaning.

There are two basic subjects that are repeated in this section. The first is the tabernacle, and the second is the covenant. In chapter 8 the author introduces the topic and states that the Tabernacle and the Covenant were simply patterns, or foreshadowings of what would be realized in Jesus. In chapter 9 he peels back the next layer of each of these topics and looks at their specifics and how they point to Jesus. In the Tabernacle the author indicates that each piece of furniture had allegorical meaning that pointed to Jesus. In the covenant the author indicates that it was necessary to use blood as the "deal-seal" to make the covenant legally binding, thus indicating one reason why Jesus had to die. Finally, in chapter 10, the author summarizes his arguments and then makes a passionate appeal for active faith in the new covenant that Jesus gives to the readers as their exalted and eternal High Priest.

Tabernacle and covenant. In order to understand the impact of chapters 8-10 we must hear those two words through the ears of the the 1st century Jew and see them through the theological lenses of the author's intended listeners. Chances are that the average Christian's idea about the tabernacle is that it is nothing more than an obscure tent-thing that Moses built that we don't need to worry about anymore (if it shows up on our radar at all). Similarly, the idea of covenant (if present at all) has been reduced to our feeble document called a contract -- a documented agreement that is legally binding but can be easily, and painlessly broken.

In chapter 8, the author introduces his basic points regarding the tabernacle and the covenant. He assumes that his readers already have a working knowledge of these two topics. He does not go into detail about them until chapter 9. Even though we do not share that intimate knowledge about the tabernacle and the covenant, I am going to follow the author's pattern and save a detailed explanation of them until next lesson. Right now we will look at the basic analogy between these two ideas and Jesus.

HEBREWS

A New Tent and a New Promise

In Exodus 25:8-9 God said to Moses, "Then have them make a sanctuary for me, and I will dwell among them. Make this tabernacle and all its furnishings exactly like the pattern I will show you. "

The word "tabernacle" simply means "tent" or dwelling place. At the time of Exodus everyone in Israel lived in a tabernacle. They were a nomadic tribe, moving through the wilderness in a tent city. When the massive group of travelers would stop they would not just plop down their gear and put up their tents wherever they wanted. Instead, they had a very methodical and precise method to setting up camp. If you were to see their camp from the sky, looking down on it, you would notice that it looked like a big plus sign. There were four spokes branching out from a center point. In each of these four spokes were 3 of the 12 tribes of Israel. Altogether the 12 tribes would radiate out from a central point. So what do you think was the central point, toward which all of their individual tents were pointing? You guessed it -- the tent of God: the Tabernacle. God pitched His tent at the center of Israelite society so that, both physically and theologically, everything in the camp would revolve around Him. At the center of God's tent was the ark which housed the physical reminder of God's promise -- His covenant -- to the nation that He would bless them and through them bless all nations.

Let's key in on the word "tent." In the opening words of John's Gospel we find a familiar passage, "the Word became flesh and made his dwelling among us." In English we lose a unique and significant connection in this verse. Literally translated it reads, "the Word became flesh and tented among us" or "pitched His tent among us." This is a strong parallel to Exodus 25:8-9. Once again God's desire is to dwell among His people. He wants to be the center of the camp, the thing toward which everyone's tent is pointed, both physically and theologically. Now, under the new order of Jesus we see that the tent is His body. God lived in a tent just like ours.

The author of Hebrews is drawing an analogy between the tent of Exodus and the body and ministry of Jesus. Next lesson we will look more closely at how the 1st century mind would have connected these two ideas through an allegorical interpretation of Scripture. For now let's let the simple analogy hang there and move to the second analogy in the chapter. Notice how the author smoothly transitions from discussion of the tabernacle to discussing the core of the tabernacle and the core of Jewish theology; the covenant.

Faith that Transcends

Once again, next lesson we will go more deeply into the idea of covenant. For now let's look at the simple explanation. In Genesis 12:1-3 God made a promise -- a covenant - to Abram. 600 years later, through his servant Moses, God gave His covenant people a set of laws to follow. These laws were designed to protect them from disease and theological distortion. Technically, these are two distinct covenants -- the covenant with Abram and the covenant with Moses -- however the people of Israel had a tendency to blend them together and make them one. This was the problem that needed to be corrected. This problem became evident quickly in the story of the nation and was a major theme in the preaching of the prophets in the Old Testament. Here the author of Hebrews reminds his readers of this fundamental truth. He quotes Jeremiah and reminds them that God promised that one day he would reestablish His laws with His people and they would bear their true intention. They would not be mere external regulations written on stone tablets and locked in a box. They would be life-transforming principles that would capture the heart and bring about spiritual transformation.

Here we are reminded of Jesus' ministry once again. Matthew captures this aspect of Jesus' teaching perfectly in the Sermon on the Mount found in Matthew 5-7. If you haven't read through that passage recently I encourage you to spend some time soaking in it this week. Here Jesus said, "I did not come to abolish the law, but to fulfill it." Jesus came to empower his people to see through external regulations of Moses' Law and see the spirit of the law -- the moral reason why -- that lies behind it.

The ministry of Jesus is not like the earthly ministry of the priests in the temple (the permanent building that took the place of the tabernacle). His covenant is not like the laws of Moses. Jesus is not about man's religion. Priestly rituals and gilded buildings have nothing to do with Jesus' mission for Earth. Jesus is about something much deeper. In the language of the 1st century, Jesus is about what happens in the Heavens as He is seated at the right hand of the throne of Majesty.

At this point we can get tripped up on the language of a throne in Heaven and "up there" and "down here." Back then people believed that there actually was a throne "up there" and a "place" where God dwelt in the "3rd Heaven" or the "celestial sphere." Unfortunately that cosmology and it corresponding metaphors have led to yet another set of distortions and physical idolatries. Today, in a world where we understand the universe to be infinite we must recalibrate our metaphors to understand the ministry of Jesus. Where is the throne of Majesty? Where is the Heavenly

HEBREWS

realm in which the true tabernacle exists and where Jesus serves as our High Priest?

It is dangerous to attempt a literal answer to that question. Many would say that the Heavenly realm truly is in our "hearts" and that God desires to "pitch his tent" in our spirit. They would be correct, but also dangerously incorrect as well. Many people today speak of the God within us in such a way that the line between us and God becomes irreversibly blurred, thus making us God. This is a distortion that can lead to serious self-indulgence and arrogance and must be avoided. Others will say that the throne of God is still "out there" somehow in a spiritual realm -- like another dimension -- into which we cannot go until we die. They would be correct and yet dangerously incorrect as well. This line of thinking is not far removed from the ancient cosmology. It simply replaces the "celestial sphere" with "another dimension" in which God dwells and is separate from us. The danger of this view is that God is disconnected from us, or more accurately, we are disconnected from God. It can lead us to the same spiritual gymnastics that happened with Gnosticism in that people believed they needed to interact with -- both in battle and in cooperation -- with the spiritual beings in order to connect with God.

The answer lies in the mystery of both ideas being right and being wrong at the same time. This is possible because they are both simply analogies and metaphors that describe something beyond our ability to understand.

The point of the message is that Jesus has "pitched His tent among us" and that we are at peace with God because of Him. He has conquered sin and death and we can trust Him. He has placed His tent in our world and invites us to point our tent toward His so that He can be the center of everything we do. The Good News of Jesus' Kingdom is not about Laws, it's about love. It's about a transformed heart that knows the love of God and does everything through and for the love of God.

Next lesson we will look more closely at the Tabernacle and the blood of the covenant.

Faith that Transcends

HEBREWS

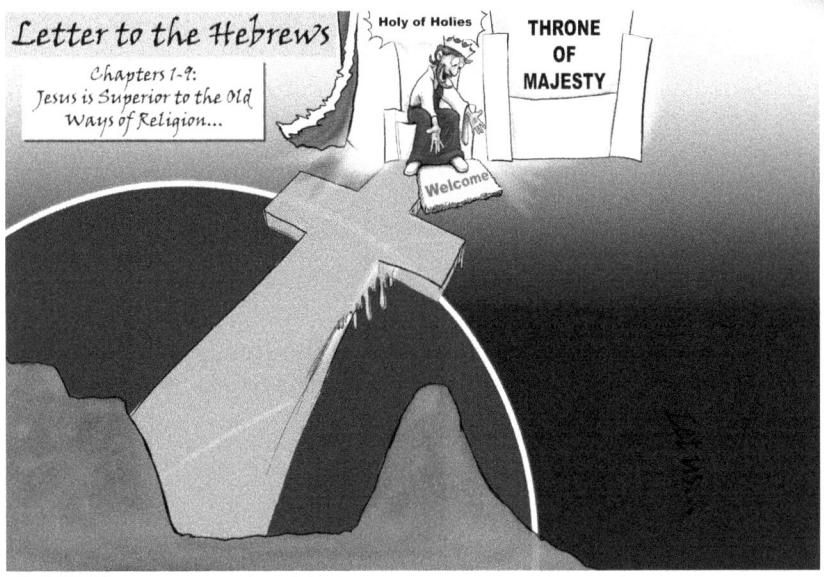

Lesson 9: Parables of Heaven

- Read Hebrews 9

Study Questions

1. Based on the description in Hebrews 9 and your reading in Exodus from the previous lesson, draw a diagram of the Tabernacle.

2. In what ways do you think this physical structure might communicate truth about the spiritual reality?

Faith that Transcends

3. According to the auhtor of Hebrews, what was the purpose of the Tabernacle?

4. In what ways was Jesus' ministry in the Heavenly Tabernacle different from the priests who served in the physical Tabernacle?

5. Read Genesis 15. What rituals did God perform in this scene?

6. Why was it necessary for Jesus to shed His blood and die?

7. How does this relate to the covenant?

HEBREWS

Food for Thought

As we discussed in the previous chapter, the author repeats his two main topics in chapter 9 and takes them down to the next level. In this chapter we see a detailed description of the layout of the tabernacle and a discussion of the importance of blood in a covenant or will.

At this point in the study there are two paths that we could take. The first would be to launch into a description of the tabernacle and the covenant of the Old Testament so that we can see the symbolism and the parallels between them and the ministry of Jesus. The second path would be to look at the overall message of the chapter and analyze the method through which the author is interpreting the tabernacle and the covenant in light of Jesus. Let's begin with the second approach before we look at the details. We will observe the forest before inspecting the trees.

Shadows, Patterns, and Parables

In Hebrews there are three key words that must be discussed in order to understand the message of the letter. The first two are found in Hebrews 8:5. They are "copy" and "shadow." The third word is found in Hebrews 9:9. It is "illustration". Let's translate these words.

"copy" is translating the Greek word "hypodeigma" which means: pattern, model, example, or copy.

"shadow" is translating the Greek word "skia" which means: shadow (this can be a literal shadow or used metaphorically)

"illustration" is translating the Greek word "parabole" which means: parable, or a story that uses a known thing to explain an unknown thing; a simile or metaphor.

While all of these words indicate the same thing, I find the word parable most intriguing. It probably jumps out at me because Jesus taught in parables. Why did he do this? Jesus came to teach us the ways of God. He came to cast a vision for us of a preferred future; a vision of what the Kingdom of God on Earth could and should look like. I don't believe He came to tell us that Heaven was "out there" and that we will never be able to reach the type of loving, God-centered world that He described. Instead I believe

Faith that Transcends

He came to plant a seed of hope and vision in us of what the world could actually look like if we would align ourselves with the spirit of God. Yet, this vision of God's Kingdom was difficult to visualize in a world plagued with human injustice, violence, and pain. It was an "unknown" that needed to be explained with a "known." Thus he spoke in parables. He used simple, ordinary things -- like sheep, trees, and sons -- to explain the deep mysterious truths of God's preferred future.

In Hebrews we see that Jesus was not doing something new. God has always been teaching us through parables. In this passage we discover that the Tabernacle itself was a parable...in 3D. The structure itself was designed to teach us important truths about the nature of God, humanity, the world and the relationship between all of those things.

At this point we must stop and ask an honest question. Which of the following is the accurate way to understand these things: a) God, in his overarching plan of revealing Himself to humanity, purposefully established the Tabernacle as a type of Christ, established 1400 years of animal sacrifice, dealt with Israel on the basis of Moses' laws, all for the purpose of paving the way for Jesus to come and show the spiritual reality behind it all, OR, b) The Laws of Moses and the Tabernacle were an organically produced, humanly constructed theological system that attempted to make sense out of Moses' authentic encounter with the infinite and was wrapped up in the theological perspective and language of the culture of that day, thus allowing the followers of Jesus to look back into those customs and recontextualize it through the lens of the reality of Jesus, using those forms as a means to communicate the mysteries of Jesus to a Jewish mind.

As you read these two options red flags and warning sirens may have gone off in your head screaming, "Liberal alert! Low view of scripture alert! Warning!" Rest assured, that is not my intent. I said this was an honest question. As you wrestle with Hebrews perhaps the following question has lurked around the corner of your mind, "If God always knew that He was going to bring Jesus on the scene, then why did He set up the Law in the first place, just to tear it down and cause so much conflict and confusion for people?" This is a fundamental question of Christian Theology and you should not feel badly about having it. It is a perennial question that has been dealt with throughout the history of the Church and every denominational movement has slight variations in their answer.

The reason I raise the question is not to throw doubt on the Bible or God's plan. I raise it to point out a very important issue in the

HEBREWS

arena of communicating the Good News of Jesus to the world. As we have said throughout this study, the letter to the Hebrews is just that...it is a letter to Hebrew/Jewish people in the 1st century. The author of Hebrews is speaking a theological and philosophical language that made perfect sense to the audience. However, you, as a non-Jew, have probably struggled through every passage trying to make sense out of it all. I raise the question because if there is any truth in option "b", then it may open up huge windows of opportunity for those of us who want to communicate the message of Jesus in our own world. Put into plain English, the question I'm raising is, "Do I have to talk about Jesus entering into the Heavenly Tabernacle and making the final sacrifice of the covenant in order to speak THE truth of Jesus to a very non-Jewish, post-Christian audience?" Another way to say it is, "is the language of SACRIFICE, BLOOD, and HIGH PRIEST an inherent truth of the absolute nature of Jesus, or is it A WAY of discussing Jesus by using Jewish language and theology as PARABLES or ANALOGIES that make connections of similarity with a cultural group in order to convey deeper truths?"

I believe we find evidence of this topic in the book of Acts as we observe the missionary journeys of Paul. When he sat down with Jews in the synagogue he quoted from the Old Testament and spoke of the Messiah. That was Jewish language. When he spoke with Greeks about Jesus he didn't do any of that. He talked in the language of the God of the Heavens and Earth who created all things. He used Greek poetry to demonstrate the truth that was present within their theology that pointed to the deeper truths of the reality of God. In the end he spoke of Justice and that God would bring about justice and peace on the Earth through Jesus. This truth was demonstrated through the resurrection of Jesus. The presentation was radically different from that given to the Jews, yet it was the same Jesus.

I bring this point up as a word of encouragement. I believe the answer to my first question is both "a" and "b". Yes, God has dealt with the nation of Israel throughout history and the scripture that records that interaction is inspired and authoritative for us all, yet, God is also at work with all people, at all times, calling them to the same preferred future of peace in the Kingdom of God. We are not called to become Jewish in order to come to Jesus. Paul made that very clear in his letters. We are called to encounter the risen Lord Jesus and be changed by the encounter and follow His teaching. Similarly, we are not called to become Christians in order to follow Jesus. We are not called to conform to ritualized forms that have become "Christian Tabernacles". We are called to encounter the risen Lord Jesus, be changed by the encounter, and follow his teachings.

Does that mean that Judaism is bad? Does that mean that Christianity is bad? Does that mean that the Tabernacle was worthless? Does that mean that the churches, doctrines, groups, and programs that we have created are bad? Not at all. We can learn so much from them. Within each of these physical things there are rich jewels to be mined and treasured as real ways to learn more about the mysterious God who loves us. I am not advocating a rejection of any of these things, in the same way that Paul did not call for a rejection of Judaism. I am simply reminding us that all of these things are "copies," "shadows," and "parables" of something much deeper and more real than anything we can imagine.

With that in mind, let's explore the other path that I mentioned at the beginning of the lesson and look at the Tabernacle and the Covenant. As we do, let's enjoy it, realizing that these things point to deep truths about Jesus, but do not fully encapsulate the truth of Jesus. The challenge for us, in our world, is to discover the touchstones in our culture that point to the truth of who Jesus is, what He taught, and how we can move toward the preferred future that He called us to strive toward.

The Tabernacle

Have you ever walked into a building and been overwhelmed with emotion simply by the architecture? Serious architects that are not just slapping up tract houses or mini-marts are artists who try to convey a message through their physical use of space and light. Their desire is to have an emotional, visceral impact on the people who enter and move through their spaces. For example, when you walk into giant stone cathedrals your eyes are instantly drawn forward to the altar and then thrust upward into the heavens. Many of these sacred spaces are domed at the top to mimic the canopy of the heavens above. These effects can also be seen in government buildings. When you enter into many of the capital buildings in our country you feel a sense of ominous presence as you are dwarfed by the domed ceilings that are supported by series of Greek columns, thus reminding you of your place in the cosmos.

HEBREWS

The tabernacle is a piece of architecture that conveys deep spiritual truths through its use of space, imagery, and furniture. Simply put, the tabernacle was a tent that was designed to be set up and torn down relatively quickly. It was used as the spiritual and literal center of the people of Israel as they moved through the wilderness just after their release from slavery in Egypt. God gave Moses specific instructions for the construction of the tabernacle in Exodus 25-40.

The tabernacle had three basic sections:

The courts. This was a space outside the main tent, but enclosed by a curtain/wall. The court contained a large basin for ceremonial washings (baptism) and an altar of fire for burning sacrifices. The people brought their offerings to the priests at the gate of the courts and watched as the priests performed the appropriate rituals with them.

Inside the tent:

The Holy Place. The first room in the tent was rectangular in shape. The entrance was at the short end of the room, facing the altar and basin on the outside. In this room were three pieces of furniture: the table, the lamp stand, and the altar of incense. On the table was placed freshly baked bread (to be refreshed every day) and pitchers for wine (used for drink offerings). The lamp stand was comprised of seven oil lamps. These lamps were to be kept perpetually burning. The altar of incense was a low, brick coal pit upon which incense would be burned in order to fill the room with smoke and aroma. The altar of incense was placed directly in front of the curtain that divided the Holy Place with the Most Holy Place.

The Most Holy Place (Holy of Holies). This room was a perfect cube and was covered with golden embroidery. In the center of the room sat the Ark of the Covenant. The ark was a wooden box covered in gold. Inside the box the stone tablets of the Law, Aaron's staff, and a jar of manna were placed, as memorials to God's eternal covenant with Israel. On the top of the box stood two, six-winged cherubim facing one another. We have discussed the Holy Place and the Mercy Seat in previous chapters.

Faith that Transcends

If you are interested in learning more about the tabernacle you can visit two interesting websites that discuss modern day replicas of it.

>http://www.bibleplaces.com/tabernacle.htm
>http://www.glencairnmuseum.org/tabernacle/index.htm

Interpretation of the Tabernacle account begins with Philo of Alexandria, the first century Jewish philosopher....To Philo, the Tabernacle served as an allegory for the cosmology of Plato. Every element of the physical abode signified a Divine reality.... the Tabernacle displays the two realms of existence. The holy of holies signifies the realm of the Divine, the realm of unchanging and perfect truth, the intelligible world as he calls it. The exact makeup and arrangement of the ark, mercy seat and cherubim in the holy of holies signifies various aspects of this realm, and more specifically, of God... The other two areas, the holy place and the courtyard, together represent the corporeal world, the world of human experience. First, the holy place, with its lamp, table and altar of incense represents the heaven of this corporeal world, and second, the courtyard, with the basin and altar of sacrifices, represent its earth.

There is another first century text that uses the method of allegory to interpret the Tabernacle, namely the book of Hebrews in the New Testament. While using the same philosophical methods, the content of Hebrews is very different from Philo's work. Here, the Tabernacle becomes a vehicle for understanding the ministry of Christ. Jesus is the true high priest, and heaven his true Tabernacle:

While these methods, borrowed from Greek philosophy, did not immediately impact rabbinic Judaism, the first centuries of Christianity were inundated with such interpretations. Early Christians, such as Origin and Clement, used both Philo and the book of Hebrews to create their own elaborate allegories for the Tabernacle. Basing themselves almost entirely on these two sources, the church fathers then made their own innovations: the sanctuary became a symbol for the soul of the individual or for the body of the church, and the Tabernacle's function to unite humanity with God became a symbol for the union of the human and Divine in Christ.

HEBREWS

Thus, interpretation of the Tabernacle in late antiquity was decidedly Greek. The method of allegorical interpretation began in the 4th century BCE with the interpretations of Homer's epics, and became so pervasive that for many it is a familiar way of reading the Bible even today. But it was during these first centuries of the Common Era that allegory truly flourished as a method for interpreting the Bible. By linking details of the Biblical stories with higher philosophical and spiritual concepts, Jews and Christians were able to incorporate their religion with the intellectual culture of the time.

(http://www.glencairnmuseum.org/tabernacle/la.htm October 28, 2006)

The Covenant

In light of our previous discussion (about option "a" and "b") it is important for us to note that the idea of a covenant was not invented at the time of God's interaction with Abram, nor is it unique to God's relationship with Abram. The truth is that God used a common practice of covenant-making in order to communicate a deep truth to Abram. In the language of Hebrews, God was using the covenant as a "parable" for Abram. In order to understand the analogies that the author of Hebrews makes between the blood of the covenant and the blood of Jesus, we must understand the nature of the ancient custom of the covenant. There is a great deal of information on this; however you probably don't want to read it all in a study like this. The following will suffice for our purposes:

We are not well informed on covenantal rites, because of lack of material. There are, however, a few vestiges of these rites left in available material. The slaughtering of an animal (sheep, donkey, bull, etc.) is described in the Mari texts, the Alalah tablets and in the Old Testament. It was the custom to cut the animal in two or three parts (so lately advocated by Cazelles). Part of it was burnt in honor of the god and part of it was eaten at a covenantal meal. In Geneis 15 such a rite is described. In Exodus 24 the same rite is mentioned. In this case the sacrifice and the covenantal meal are clearly described. In certain ancient Near Eastern vassal treaties it is stated that the vassal is compelled to visit the great king annually to renew the treaty. Although the Old Testament is not clear on this point, it is not unlikely that the same custom existed in Israel. It is possible that the Israelites gathered with a certain festival (New Year's festival) to renew the covenant.

The point of all this is that blood was a very important aspect of the covenant. Something had to die and its blood had to be used to cleanse the people involved in the agreement. Why was this? We aren't sure, exactly. However, there are two points that may be helpful for us. First, the death of an animal signalled the intensity and importance of the agreement. This was not just some whimsical flight of fancy that two passers-by felt like getting into. This was a life-pact that held grave consequences. The agreement between a lord and a vassal held life and death issues at stake. It was an agreement that could not be entered into lightly. Secondly, death reminds us of the severity of our condition apart from God. Sin has caused things to run amuck and its consequence is death and despair in the world. The death of an animal reminds the parties of the state of affairs and compels them to move toward a more preferred future.

Jesus came to bring a new covenant. This is Jewish language. He came to bring peace. If you were making a covenant you had to have blood. In explaining Jesus' death to a person who operated under the worldview of covenant, then it made sense to point to the blood of Jesus as the "deal-sealer" for the covenant.

Here's the question for us: Is it the blood of Jesus that we worship? Is there magical power in the physical blood of Jesus? Or, is the blood a symbol for something deeper. For the covenant person it represented a sealed deal. For other people it may represent the life of a body. For others it may represent a self-sacrificial death that demonstrates ultimate love. Once again, the blood is just a part of the whole package of the Gospel. The Good News lies in the reality that Jesus "tented" among us, taught us how to live, cast a vision of a preferred future, demonstrated His love and the sincerity of God's commitment to us through His death, and demonstrated His power and His right to be called the true "Lord" or "Ruler" or "Emperor" or "Leader" of all things through His bodily resurrection.. Today He stands as the Lord and invites us to his Kingdom as He "sits at the right hand of the Throne of Glory." We thank God for these "parables" found in history that stand as tangible "copies" of a deep mysterious truth that is real and accessible to all who believe and enter in.

May we look past our copies and fix our eyes on Jesus. May we follow His example and hold to His teaching, and in so doing help propel our world toward the vision of his preferred future.

HEBREWS

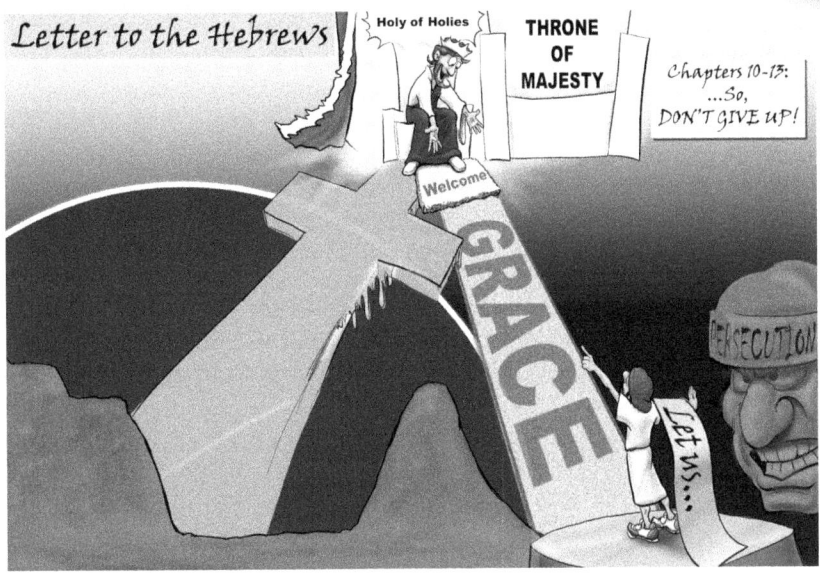

Lesson 10: More Salad

- Read: Hebrews 10

Study Questions

1. Read Psalm 40. List the attitudes of the writer toward God in the Psalm.

2. How does the section quoted in Hebrews fit in the context of the whole Psalm?

3. What is the point of the Hebrew author in quoting this passage?

Faith that Transcends

4. Make a list of the things the author encourages the readers to "let us" do.

5. Take a few moments to review this list. Rate yourself on these items. In which of them are you feeling strong. Which ones need work? Why? What could you do to grow in these areas?

6. How had the readers behaved previously in the face of temptation and persecution? What does the author warn them against this time? Why? What is at stake?

7. What is your emotional to this warning passage? What is your intellectual response (what questions does it raise for you)?

HEBREWS

Food for Thought:

Concluding Remarks: The Message has always been there. (1-18)

The first verses of this chapter are actually the concluding words of the last few chapters. They are like the closing argument of a trial lawyer as he tries to convince the jury that his position is one built upon sound reasoning. Basically he is saying, "Look, what I'm telling you is not new. It has always been there. A relationship with God has never been about external regulations; it has always been about the condition of a person's heart."

We can see this to be true as we track with the examples he gives in the letter:

- ◇ we saw it with Abraham in his relationship with God through Melchizedek. Abraham had no law but was right before God simply because he believed God to be true.
- ◇ we saw it with Moses on the mountain. He was able to go into the mysterious presence of God on the mountain while the people simply saw a scary lightning show. Moses could enter the Tent of Meeting directly, but the people had to hang at the gate to the courtyard while the priests burned their sacrifices for them.
- ◇ we see it in David's relationship with God and his attitude toward the regulations. Throughout David's life we see him engaged in a dynamic relationship with God, seemingly above the law. He exposed the truth of the sacrifices in Psalm 40: they mean nothing if the heart is not right.
- ◇ we see it in the lives of the prophets. They always stood outside the camp and looked in. Isaiah and Jeremiah -- both heavily quoted in Hebrews -- saw through the trappings of the temple and the circumstances of war, pestilence, and violence, and saw the vision of God's preferred future when people's hearts were authentically in communion with God and living in peace with one another.

Jesus came to make this point crystal clear. God wants our hearts. He wants to make our hearts pure because He knows that out of a pure heart come pure motives and behaviors. He wants our hearts to be captured by His love, transformed by it, and overflowing with it to everyone we meet. That is why Jesus came. He taught it, he lived it, He demonstrated it, and He delivers it. Because of that, you can count on it.

The Big Salad (19-25)

In these 7 verses we come to another salad bowl in Hebrews. The last one was found in chapter 4. In that chapter the author challenged the readers by saying, "lettuce...I mean...Let us, therefore, make every effort to enter that rest, so that no one will fall by following their example of disobedience." In that chapter he was concluding his argument regarding the fact that Jesus was higher than the angels, Moses, and the Sabbath Rest. Then in 4:14-16 he transitions to a deeper topic by saying,

> "Since we have a great High Priest who has gone through the heavens, Jesus the Son of God, let us hold firmly to the faith we profess. For we do not have a high priest who is unable to sympathize with our weaknesses, but we have one who has been tempted in every way, just as we are—yet was without sin. Let us then approach the throne of grace with confidence, so that we may receive mercy and find grace to help us in our time of need."

Do you see the direct parallel to our current passage? Hebrews 4:14-16 and 10:18-25 are bookend passages. Everything from 5:1-10:17 has been the author's exposition of what it means to call Jesus our High Priest. In this passage we get to the point of it all. Now we answer the question, "So what?" This passage is the true heart of the letter. Everything before it is a theological foundation upon which to launch this challenge and everything after it is a warning to not ignore this challenge. As we discussed last lesson, his argumentation and theological construction may have been foreign to you. Perhaps, in our day, we need to develop a slightly different approach to constructing an argument that will connect with the modern/post-modern, post-industrial, western mind. Regardless of that, no matter how we construct the argument, we will reach the same conclusion -- Jesus is the Lord of all things and WE CAN PUT OUR TRUST IN HIM!

In this great truth our worlds -- that of Hebrews and our contemporary culture -- can converge as we read the very practical challenge that the author sets before his readers. As you explore these four topics I encourage you to enter them with a spirit of openness to God's instruction. Ask Him to expose really practical ways in which you can grow in these areas.

HEBREWS

Let us...

draw near to God

There are two important points here. First of all, it is possible to draw near to God. God is real and God desires to be in relationship with you. Secondly, your heart has been made clean. The tense of the Greek verbs here is the perfect passive. That means something has happened to you in the past. It is not something you did, nor is it an ongoing thing. God sprinkled you. God cleared your record. Put in our language, God has forgiven you and doesn't hold anything against you. He is your Father. He loves you. He desires for you to walk in His love and enjoy the peace that comes from being at peace with everyone, even your enemies.

At this point there may be a new stumbling block that could emerge for Christians. Many people who love Jesus and believe He is who He says He is and have strong faith in Him have never felt a special presence. They've never been caught up to the 3rd Heaven like Paul. They've never gotten all tingly and jumped around. They've never spoken in tongues or healed people. For them it has simply been belief. Unfortunately, there has been a great movement with the body of Christ that has caused those with simple faith to doubt whether they really believe. They ask, "What does it really mean to enter God's presence with confidence? Am I supposed to do something, or feel something? Maybe those other people know something I don't." If you are a person who does feel all tingly or speak in tongues, then praise God and good for you. I'm not trying to discredit your experience. You can tune out now. If you are the kind of person I've been describing then I want to encourage you right now. You don't have to tingle to believe. God's presence isn't a "place" where you go, nor is it a certain prescribed experience you must have. God's presence is a present reality. It is the knowledge that God is real, that He loves you, and that your relationship is good. Sometimes that kind of deep faith is the kind of faith that can weather the storm. Shallow water is turbulent and strong winds can vaporize it. Still waters run deep and neither wind nor ice can disturb it. Don't allow modern "externals" -- no matter what they are -- distract you from simple faith. That is all God asks....believe.

hold unswervingly to hope

Here we see the real by-product of faith. We don't have faith so that we can put on a great religious show. We don't have faith so that we can do great things or have transcendental experiences. We have faith so that we can have hope. When it is all said and done, hope is all we really have. Throughout the Bible we are taught that "the rain falls on the evil and the good." Circumstances come and circumstances go. Sometimes good people suffer and bad people prosper. Sometimes hard work pays off, sometimes you fail. Sometimes eating right and exercise brings about great health, sometimes fitness advocates drop dead of a heart attack while running. Sometimes good parenting produces quality adults, and sometimes kids rebel for no apparent reason. If our state of well being was dependent upon our circumstances then we would be a wreck. We would get motion sickness on the roller coaster that is called life. But, if we believe in a higher way of being -- following the ethics and teachings of Jesus -- then we know there is more. When we hook our anchor into the vision of God's Kingdom where people can and will walk in the love of God and live at peace with God, humans, and all creation, then we can have hope. We can have an "eternal perspective" (meaning to see things from a God-perspective, not a human-perspective) and know that all things can be used to bring about transformation in people, if we only let them. Everything, no matter how bleak, can be a teachable moment if we see through Jesus lenses. When we realize that, then we can have hope. This hope is not wishful thinking. This hope is in the reality of Jesus. He lived it, taught it, demonstrated it, and perpetuates it eternally for us. That is hope.

consider how we may spur one another on toward love and good deeds

Now we get to the really practical part of the discussion. If God's Kingdom is a Kingdom of love and peace where every person looks to the best interest by working to bring about the best for the world as a whole, then it only makes sense that the primary purpose of the church is to be a catalytic community in which we spur one another one towards love in action. Simply put, don't just talk about it -- demonstrate it.

The Greek word translated "spur" is the word "paraxsusmos". It literally means to provoke to anger or to irritate. The author uses an ironic mixture of words as he encourages the church to "irritate one another to love and good deeds." The proverb "As iron sharpens iron, so one man sharpens another" (Proverbs 27:17) comes to mind. Let's face it, sometimes we get comfortably lazy. In a world full of such global crisis it is easy to numb out and convince yourself that you can't really make a difference anyway. One of the most important reasons for the church to commit to the discipline of gathering together is to "irritate" one another toward love.

Accountability is essential. When we think of accountability we generally think of a person who has fallen into sin and needs someone to keep him on the straight and narrow. While that is a very necessary reality, it is only a part of the scope of accountability. Perhaps we need to take a more proactive approach to the process of "positive irritation." When we gather in our intimate communities we should be asking about how our relationships are going. Are we loving our family members? Are we being quick to listen and slow to anger? Are we making time to invest in others rather than burning the candle at both ends for a paycheck? Are we looking outside our comfort zone and asking God where we can touch the life of a hurting and needy person? Are we finding ways that we, as a community, can become involved in the global community and truly be salt and light in the world? Sometimes a little prodding, a little holy burr under the saddle from a loving brother or sister is just what we need to keep focused and keep our head in the game.

not give up meeting together

I think this phrase means more than "go to church." There are many people who have shown up in the building every Sunday of their lives but have never gone to church. First of all, church is not a place you attend. It is something you are. The church is the family of God. As we discussed in the previous section, the church must meet together if it is going to be "irritating" to one another.

For the original reader of Hebrews this challenge carried more weight than it does for us today. Remember, they were being persecuted. For them to gather together was dangerous. It would have been easy for them to rationalize the decision to disband the gathering. "Hey, we don't need the church to be able to talk to God, right? It's safer if we just commune with him in the privacy of our own home." That decision would be disastrous for the church. What would happen if the church stopped gathering?

Everyone would be alone. They would be isolated. Isolation is Hell. Organic things don't grow in isolation. Iron becomes dull in isolation. Thoughts become rigid and stale in isolation. Trees become sterile and unfruitful in isolation. If we as individuals, if we as the church, if we as the world are going to be strong and healthy, then we need to meet together. We need to bump up against each other. We need to be in unity, but we also need to disagree and sharpen each other. We need to cross-pollinate ideas and allow the seed of the Kingdom of God to be watered by the Spirit and grow into something new and fresh in every generation -- in every day.

Perhaps you are discouraged by the state of the church. Perhaps you feel like you are the only crazy one out there and you just don't fit into the churches that you've been visiting. Perhaps you feel like the church you are in is running cold, or stale, or just going through the motions. Don't give up! Be a positive irritant. Be honest. Raise tough questions. Whatever you do, don't forsake being together. When that happens we are lost. We fall into the pit of isolation and the roots of despair may choke us out. Even if it is two or three people meeting in a coffee shop in the name of Jesus, don't give up. Put your hope in Jesus. Spur one another on!

Don't Give Up! (26-39)

This section raises huge theological questions. The biggest question is whether it is possible to "lose your salvation." There are basically two schools of thought on this issue. Some say that it is possible to "be saved" at one point in life and then to "not be saved" at a later point because you choose to walk away from faith. Others say that it is impossible to "lose your salvation" and that people who apparently walk away from faith were never really "saved" in the first place.

Before we can resolve that issue (if we can) we must acknowledge that this whole discussion begs a more fundamental question: what does it mean to be "saved." On this broader question there are three basic camps. The first camp believes that everyone is born lost because of sin in the world and bound for Hell and that only those people who follow a certain Christian ritual -- be baptized, pray the sinners prayer, join the church, etc. -- are "saved" from eternal life in Hell because of God's Grace. (within that camp they argue about who gets saved; do you have to be "elect" or can anybody choose to be saved) The second camp is

HEBREWS

like the first in that they believe everyone is born lost and is bound for Hell, but, because of God's grace, everyone is allowed into Heaven, e.g. everyone is "saved." The third camp believes that, because of God's Grace, everyone is made clean through the work of Jesus, but that, because of God's Grace and Justice, everyone is allowed the opportunity to "opt out" of God's Grace and rebel against him.

With those three camps in mind, let's look at this passage in Hebrews. According to the words of the author, it seems entirely possible for a person to be a follower of Jesus and then to turn away from Him. This was a very real problem for the Hebrew readers. They were being forced by the Romans to choose between recanting, or denouncing Jesus as Lord, and death. What are the implications for a person who willingly says, "No, I don't believe that Jesus is the Lord? I worship Caesar as Lord. Jesus is just another god among many." Is it possible for that person to truly be in authentic relationship with God? Is it possible for that person to live in both belief systems: Yes, I believe Jesus is Lord and I want to live in His Kingdom AND No, I don't believe Jesus is Lord and I reject Him as King? It is not possible.

Here's an important point. In this scenario, who is rejecting whom? Does God look down and say, "You blew it buddy, I'm throwing you out?" Or, does the human look up into the face of God and say, "I know you invited me in and it's a done deal, but I want out?" If that person walks away he turns from having the light of God's presence on his face (metaphorically) and faces into the shadow. He is lost, He is isolated. He is in Hell.

Here's the real question. Can that person ever come back? Based upon the core of the Gospel message, it seems to me that he could. If he repented -- changed his mind and turned around -- then God's plan and invitation would still be the same. Jesus paid the price, the curtain is torn open, and He has sprinkled us. Perhaps the author of Hebrews is saying to his people, "Do you really want to go through that? Do you really want to slap God in the face by snubbing His grace and drag Him through all this mess again, just because you're scared? Be stronger than that. If you turn away now, the shame you experience may be so great you'll never lift up your eyes to God again. Don't run the risk."

Let's get back to the theological question. Of the three camps discussed -- 1. everyone's out until they ask to get in, 2. everyone's out, but God lets everyone in, 3. everyone's in, but God let's anyone "opt out." -- which one adequately handles this passage? Numbers 1 and 3 do. This passage in Hebrews points to some level of truth to the idea that it is possible to walk away from God.

At this point we are going to leave the rest of the issue hanging in healthy tension. If you are intrigued by the topic, do some theological research in the area of "soteriology" or the study of salvation.

For now let me leave you with some comfort. While I do believe it is possible to walk away from God, I don't believe it is possible to "lose your salvation." When people speak of losing salvation they are generally referring to sin management. In other words, they believe that if you sin then you aren't saved and are going to Hell. So, you must constantly manage your sin and make sure that you are "paid up" in your confessions to God. Otherwise, you might just wake up in eternity on the wrong side of the equation. I believe that kind of thinking regarding sin and God's grace is dangerous and diametrically opposed to the Gospel. If we've learned nothing else from Hebrews we have learned that Jesus paid for our sins. They're gone. It's done. You don't have to make sin offerings everyday. He did it and you are at peace with God. He loves you. Yes, you will struggle with sin and will stumble and bumble on the path of sanctification -- being made clean and holy through a process of growth -- but that is part of the growing process.

As a parent I don't throw my child out of the family when she falls down. I help her get up and teach her not to fall. However, if my daughter looks me in the eye and says, "I hate you and I'm leaving," then walks out the door, never to be seen again, what can I do? I still love her, but she has removed herself from me.

The Gospel message is a message of hope, not fear. God loves you. He wants you to grow. Believe it. Then let him change you. Be at peace.

HEBREWS

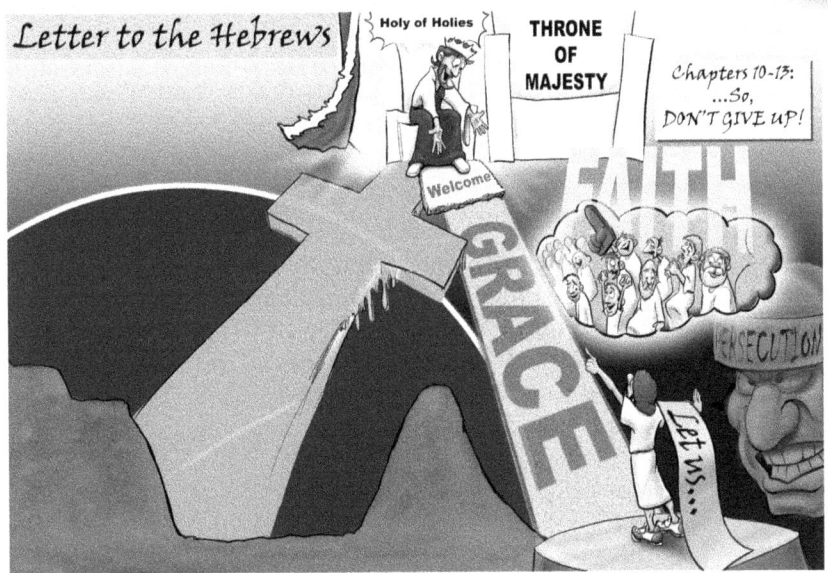

Lesson 11: The Story of Faith

- Read: Hebrews 11

Study Questions

1. Read Hebrews 10:35-39. Paraphrase this passage in your own words.

2. Read Habakkuk (it's only three short chapters). Look at Habakkuk 2:4. In the context of the whole message of Habakkuk, what does this verse mean?

Faith that Transcends

3. Why does the author of Hebrews quote Habakkuk 2:4 at the end of Hebrews 10? What message is he trying to communicate?

4. As you read through the list of people mentioned in chapter 11, make a note of the characters that you are not familiar with. Go back and read their stories in the Old Testament. Spend some time soaking in the stories of these people. What is God teaching you through their lives?

5. How does the author of Hebrews characterize these people? What makes them worthy of noting? What is the transferrable principle, or example, from their lives that the author wants to present to his readers?

6. In what aspect of your life do you need to be more like these people? Why?

7. What message have you heard from this chapter that God is trying to communicate to you?

Food for Thought

The Springboard

Before we dive into chapter 11 we must back up and get a running start in chapter 10:35. Chapter 11 is the evidence for the statement made in these verses. Verses 37-38 are a loose quotation from the Old Testament prophet Habakkuk. Therefore, in order to understand the meaning of this passage we must first visit this prophet and find out what was going on when he penned these words.

Habakkuk was a man who lived in Jerusalem. During his life he watched as the empire of Babylon pressed closer and closer toward Jerusalem. From this Jewish man's perspective, Babylon was a wicked nation that was the very embodiment of evil and everything opposed to the ways of God. The short book of Habakkuk is actually a conversation between the prophet and God. Allow me to paraphrase the conversation:

> Hab: God, I'm tired of dealing with the corruption of Israel. How long do I have to put up with this?
>
> God: Check this out. You won't believe what I'm about to do. I'm going to use Babylon to bring judgment on Israel. Yep, they're going to come in and clean house.
>
> Hab: What?!? Excuse me. Did I hear you right? You are going to use *them*? They are wicked. They hate you. They represent everything that is opposed to you. Their violence and corruption makes our corruption look like good deeds. I thought you were holy and faithful to your people. How could you do something like this?
>
> God: Don't worry. Just wait and see. My Kingdom and My Justice will always prevail in the end. I'm not saying I'm condoning Babylon. Their pride will be their own undoing. What I am saying is that 1) I'm in control of all nations, and 2) Being a nation is not what saves you. What saves you is faith. Believe in Me. Follow my ways, no matter what is going on around you. If you do, you will be able to rise above your circumstances like a deer that climbs up to a high place of safety.

Faith that Transcends

Here are some observations from Habakkuk:

1. It is OK to question God. It is OK to not understand what is happening. It is OK to not be OK with what seems to be rampant injustice. God can handle your honesty. As long as you are coming to Him in honest and authentic questioning, He says, "Bring it on." What God doesn't want is empty religiosity. He wants a dynamic and honest heart that pursues Him and wrestles with Him as it seeks to know truth and live out justice in the world.

2. Often times the reality of life flies upside down in relation to the ways of God. More often than not the wicked prevail. The history of humanity is dominated by the stories of empires running rampant across weaker nations, suppressing them and extorting them. Even though this is the dominant theme of the human story, it is not the vision of God's preferred Kingdom.

3. The Kingdom of God runs concurrent with the perversion of human governments. It is both concurrent and transcendent. In plain English, the Kingdom of God is populated by people of all nations who, by faith, follow the ways of God. Those who seek justice, and love mercy, and walk humbly with God, in spite of the climate in which they live, are the ones who see the vision of God's preferred future and cling to it.

4. Habakkuk 2:4 is a key verse for understanding the New Testament. It is quoted in Romans 1:17, Galatians 3:11, and Hebrews 10:38. The key phrase is "the righteous will live by faith." The term 'righteous" and 'righteousness" (translating "dikaiosune") refers to faithfulness to a promise. God is "righteous" in that He remains faithful to His covenant with Israel even when Israel is unfaithful to Him. In a sense, the phrase reads, "the faithful one will live by faith." The word 'faith" (translating "pisteuo") means to place trust in something; to believe. The key to "salvation" is to believe that God is faithful. No matter what the circumstances -- whether it is Babylon coming to devour your city, or Rome threatening to destroy your family, or a global empire threatening to exploit your people, or a "bully" taking advantage of you -- we must believe that God is in control and that His justice will ultimately prevail. When we live by faith and simply follow

HEBREWS

the laws of God -- the law to love God and love our neighbor -- then we will be able to transcend the circumstances of our cultural situation and claim the words of Habakkuk 3:19 as our own;

The Sovereign LORD is my strength; he makes my feet like the feet of a deer, he enables me to go on the heights.

What is Faith?

Now, let's get back to Hebrews. In light of the circumstances of the Hebrew readers it makes sense that the author would quote this passage from Habakkuk. Rome had become the new Babylon for the Jews. A corrupt Empire was oppressing God's people and it seemed that injustice was prevailing. They were most likely asking of God the same question that Habakkuk was asking, "Why God? Why are you letting this happen? I thought Jesus was Lord. I thought He came to make it all better. How long must I wait to see your justice on Earth? I don't know if I can stand up any longer under the oppression of this regime."

You can hear the passion as the author responds, "We are not of those who shrink back and are destroyed, but of those who believe and are saved!!!" "We will overcome! We must have faith!"

There is our key word: FAITH. What is faith? "Faith is being sure of what we hope for and certain of what we do not see." From this point on the author expounds upon the idea of faith by listing a "great cloud of witnesses" from Israel's history that were examples of the kind of faith he is talking about.

Rather than walk through each person in this list, I'd like to spend our time on another path. I think it is important for us to look closely at the definition of faith presented above and make sure we really understand it.

What is it that we hope for, and how can we be certain of it? What do we not see? How can we be certain of what we do not see when we can't see it? Let's be honest. This sounds like fairy tale material. If you go to Disneyland you will hear a polished narrator speak the words "just believe" over the sound of beautiful instruments and you may be inspired. It seems that most of the movies made for children today camp on the idea of 'belief' with messages like, "all you have to do is believe." While this is a good and positive message, it leaves us with the question, "believe in what?" What is the object of our faith? This question is especially difficult for a mind that has been formed by the modern western model of empirical science. We have been trained that we cannot believe something unless it is physically present and able to be proven through the scientific method. It is ludicrous and superstitious to believe in something that is beyond the human senses. This dominant idea has led to two groups of people in the West. First there are people who are complete naturalists. Through reason and science they have completely done away with the possibility of any kind of "extra-sensory perception." They claim that their faith is in their own ability to perceive and they will only believe what they can see. In light of this perspective the Hebrews 11:1 definition of faith is relegated to superstitious talk of ancient people living in the dark ages. The second group of people is those who, observing the emptiness of the naturalist "soul", have rejected that perspective and have opened themselves up to the potential of "extra-sensory perception" of any kind. They have inverted the modern phrase "seeing is believing" to "believing is seeing". They believe that the human ability to perceive has creative power and that we have the ability to "create our own realities" by simply believing them to be true and then living in them. This group of people would take the Hebrews 11:1 definition of faith and fully embrace it as the core of their Gospel. Yet, the object of their faith and the thing not seen is a figment of their own imagination, thus placing them in the position of God as the creator of realities.

While these were not necessarily the same questions the original readers of Hebrews were asking, they are similar. They questioned the nature of the object of their faith. They needed to know the reason behind their willingness to die. Even though our cultural questions and circumstances may be different, we, too, ask these questions in a modern/post-modern era. How does the follower of Jesus navigate these current waters of faith? First of all, we must acknowledge the truth in both camps. We need to agree with the modernist that we cannot "prove" anything that exists beyond our human senses. If God is real, then God is infinite and is, by definition, completely beyond our ability to perceive within the boundaries of our limited self. If anyone tries to "prove" the existence of God through modern scientific terms, then all he will do is "prove" atheism, because, according to the limitations of the scientific method, God does not exist. However, we must also strongly disagree with the modernist and acknowledge the incredibly limited scope of the scientific method. Science itself has pointed to the reality that there are things in the universe -- physical things like electromagnetic radiation and sub-sub atomic particles -- that are beyond the scope of our physical senses.

HEBREWS

The universe is apparently infinite and to believe that all of reality is bound by my ability to perceive it is ludicrous. We must be open to the unknown and be willing to embrace the mystery: mystery, not in the sense of a puzzle that my ability to reason simply has not yet figured out, but mystery in the sense that I cannot know it within the limitation of my ability to perceive.

On this point we move to the other camp and come into agreement with them. We need to celebrate the intuitive truth that this group has courageously championed in our naturalistic world. Since the dawn of the Enlightenment there has been a resistance underground of poets, artists, and philosophers that have rejected the boundaries of empirical science and have embraced the unknown. This group has kept our imaginations alive and has been the fertilizer for our souls in an age of sterile knowledge. It is this group that has acknowledged creativity and imagination as an authentic and vital part of what it means to be created in the image of God. This group has not been afraid to challenge the status quo and "think outside the box", thus breathing new life into stale institutions -- new wine into old wine skins. We, as followers of Jesus, should embrace the mystery that this group has kept alive, but we should also proceed with caution. There is a line that we need to be careful not to cross. Granted the line is fuzzy, being more of a caution zone than a clear demarcation. Yet, we must not cross into the complete subjectivism of this group. When taken to its logical extreme, this group falls into a dangerous world of distorted pantheism where all is one and "god" is not a someone to be known, but simply a non-personal force that binds all things together, thus making my will equivalent to god's will. In this perspective we can be deluded to think that we can actually create our own reality by simply believing it to be true. I say this is a "zone" because there is some truth to the notion that our belief does have power over our state of well-being. After all, Jesus taught us that we have to believe in order be in the Kingdom that He presented. God has endowed us with some control over our own ability to perceive and process our circumstances. Yet, saying that does not mean that by believing we create the Kingdom of God, or Jesus, or anything. It simply means we have the power to either agree with, or disagree with the mysterious reality that Jesus presented that is both knowable and outside of our ability to perceive.

What do we hope for?

With that modern/post-modern contextual analysis behind us, let's now ask the simple question. What is the object of our faith? What do we hope for that is not seen? It is safe to say that all Christians, both now and through time would agree on the answer to that question. We hope for the Kingdom of God that is not seen. That has been the whole point of Hebrews. The author has demonstrated for us that Jesus has transcended the religiosity of the Old Testament and has entered into the eternal Holy of Holies in order to make the one, eternal sacrifice for sin. He has ripped open the dividing curtain and has invited each of us to come boldly before the throne of Grace and to live in the Kingdom of God. Now, the next question must be asked. What is the Kingdom of God? Here Christians have differed in response. Traditionally -- especially within the last 400 years of Protestantism at least -- the dominant answer to that question has been a future hope. The interpretation goes like this:

> In Hebrews 10:38, when the author says, "He who is coming will come and will not delay," he is referring to the second coming of Jesus. When Habakkuk, and all the prophets, wrote they saw two days in mind. They saw their own day, but they also saw the day when the Messiah would come and establish His kingdom on earth forever. The writers of the New Testament shared a similar vision. They understood the hope of the nations to rest in the coming of a victorious Messiah. The first coming of the Messiah was the suffering servant who bled and died for our sins. But the second coming of the Messiah will be different. The hope of the believer is the second coming of Jesus. When He returns then He will bring justice on the earth because He will be the King and everyone will have to bow their knee to Him. This is not seen because it has not yet happened. The faithful heroes listed in chapter 11 were looking forward to this day, but they never saw it. So too, do we look forward to this future glorious day. We may die before He returns, but we must pass that hope on to our children.

While this has been the dominant view, there is an alternative perspective that is worth examining.

> When the author quotes Habakkuk, the coming to which he referred was not the ultimate coming of the Messiah to establish an eternal Kingdom on earth, but the coming of

HEBREWS

the empire of Babylon to wreak havoc on Israel within the context of the prophecy and conversation that Habakkuk was having with God. Enfolded within that coming was also the destruction of the empire of Babylon, thus demonstrating God's justice in that the destroyer would be destroyed because God is in control of all things.

The message in Habakkuk, and the message in Hebrews was that God's justice and His plan are bigger than any one nation. Nations will rise in terror and corruption and wreak havoc on good people. Then those nations will meet their just end as they implode upon themselves. This is the pattern of sin within humanity. However, those who live by faith, being established on the reality of God that transcends the corrupt and self-annihilating patterns of human society, will be free of this corruption -- will be "saved" -- and be able to hold on to the hope of a better society that is possible when people follow the ways of God.

When Jesus came, He was the Messiah, completely. He did bring victory over sin and evil human regimes. He didn't do it with a sword; He did it with humility and peace. He did it through love as He laid down His life for His friends -- us. In His teaching, death, and resurrection Jesus brought with Him the Kingdom of God. He demonstrated for us what it actually looks like to live the way God wants us to live in the real world. He invites us to follow His example and live that way today, in the Kingdom of God right now.

The people listed in Hebrews 11 were heroes because they had a dynamic relationship with God. Even though their world was filled with pain and suffering, they looked to the future hope of a world where people walked with God. Since the time of Jesus there have also been heroes that have kept the hope alive by living simple, humble lives of love and peace in a world of hatred and strife. They did this even when people hated them and killed them for their walk of faith.

The author of Hebrews passionately pleaded with his people to not give in to fear and self-protection but to hold on to the substance of the reality of Jesus' way of living in the shadow of a destructive regime. He calls to us as well. He urges us to live lives that demonstrate the peace that comes through knowing God and being filled with His love.

So, which one of these perspectives is right? Is our hope solely in the future coming of the King when He will kick sinners' butts and set things in order? Or, is our hope in the humble living out of the love of God in the world demonstrated by Jesus' life and empowered by His indwelling Spirit? The truth, of course, lies in the fact that it is both and neither. If it were one or the other then we would be ultimately left hanging. If it were only the first perspective then we have no real reason for living now and no good explanation for why God created the world. If the world is so messed up then why did God make it in the first place? Why does He wait so long to return? The future-only perspective tends to lead people to devalue the present life and the present creation. Many well-intentioned Christians have embraced a doctrine of hatred toward "sinners" and toward nature under the premise that "hey, it's all going to burn anyway, right?"

If the Kingdom is only now, in this life, then we have some problems as well. This thinking can lead to an existentialist perspective that denies the afterlife and sees no true value in anything. If it is only now and only the present situation as it is, then we could quickly become disillusioned and lose hope or motivation.

The answer lies in the middle; in the both-and. All of creation is good. God's Kingdom is for right now. Jesus instituted a pattern of living right now and invited us into His project of renovating our hearts and making us into the kind of people that can know God more fully. He created us to be stewards of the planet, to care for all things, to protect the weak and vulnerable, to heal the sick, to promote justice in human affairs, and to love all things with God's love. He promised that He would be with us and would empower us with His Spirit to live like this, right now, in the real world. It is the purpose of the church to encourage and empower people to walk with Jesus toward this vision of the preferred future; to continually realize the dream that Jesus placed in our hearts. Yet, Jesus also promised that He would return. We don't know when. We don't know how, but He did say it. I don't think this return gives us hope for the Kingdom of God in the sense that the future-only perspective does, rather, I think it gives us hope in eternal life beyond the grave. When we die we will be able to continue the journey toward the ever-deepening understanding of the nature of God. That is something to look forward to. However, it is not a vision that gets us off the hook in our present existence and allows us to let the world destroy itself. Our faith is in the reality that the Kingdom of God -- the way of Jesus -- is a present possibility and is available for all who want to engage in the process of being transformed and participating in transforming society through love and peace.

Final thoughts

Before we conclude this lesson there are two verses that I'd like to highlight.

A Fresh Gospel

In verse 6 we see a version of the Gospel that is desperately needed in our world. The author said that Enoch was taken up with God because he pleased God. In explaining how to please God he gives us some rich words that we can chew on for a while. He said, "Without faith it is impossible to please God, because anyone who comes to Him must believe that He exists and that He rewards those who earnestly seek Him." Too many times our version of the gospel, and our definition of salvation says, "God will only let you into Heaven if you have all of your doctrine in order and believe exactly the right teaching about God, Jesus, creation, sin, etc. If you don't believe these things, say the right words, or join the right church, then you will burn in Hell forever." Those are scary words that don't seem to carry much "Good News" in them. As a corrective, perhaps we should dwell more on verse 6.

God rewards those who diligently seek Him. God wants to be known by His creation, that's why He created us. Perhaps many of the people whom the church condemns because they ask tough questions about the church have more faith than the church. As this verse tells us, it takes faith to even be able to ask the questions. If the person had no faith, they wouldn't even care. They would just go with whatever culture they found themselves in and slide happily into oblivion. But the person who cares enough to stop and ask tough questions is actually demonstrating faith -- belief -- that there is something more to it all. They truly want to know God and are not afraid to ruffle feathers to get there.

If a person is truly seeking God, they will find Him. Perhaps they may even find an aspect of God that is truer than the God we have constructed and worship within our own ghettos of Christianity.

As the church, we should not shun the true seeker. Perhaps we should join them on their quest. At the very least we should embrace them and contribute to their quest.

Faith that Transcends

Things not seen

The final thought for this lesson takes us to verse 39. All of these heroes of chapter 11 were commended for their faith, yet none of them received what had been promised. In a world of microwave ovens, fast food, and high speed downloads, we have become addicted to instant gratification. There is not a lot of faith required when we get what we hope for in 30 seconds or less. Many of us become weary in doing good, as Paul put it in Galatians 6:9.

Perhaps you are raising children. You have spent the last 10-20 years of your life trying to train your children to walk in love and respect for others, to work hard, and to be responsible. You have sacrificed sleep, and career, and personal gain so that your children would have what they need, and now they are adolescents and you are an idiot. Have faith. Hold on to hope. Don't give up.

Perhaps you have lived with integrity at work and have always served the company and others with humility and now you are getting passed over for the promotion or are being laid off. Have faith. Hold on to hope. Don't give up.

Perhaps you have worked hard to build a ministry or an organization that promotes the love of Jesus or justice in the world and the people around you have grown cold or turned on you. Have faith. Hold on to hope. Don't give up.

Perhaps you have lived a clean and healthy life, but now you have been faced with the reality of cancer. Have faith. Hold on to hope. Don't give up.

Jesus' Kingdom is bigger than all those things. Faith is the substance of things hoped for, the evidence of things not seen. The love of Jesus is like a seed. When we plant it we may not see it grow for a long time. We can cultivate it and water it, but it may lay dormant for a painfully long time. But, don't give up. The love of Jesus and the Justice of God will prevail. No matter the circumstances, when we act justly and love mercy and walk humbly with God then we can rest assured that we live in the Kingdom of God and the gates of Hell will not prevail.

HEBREWS

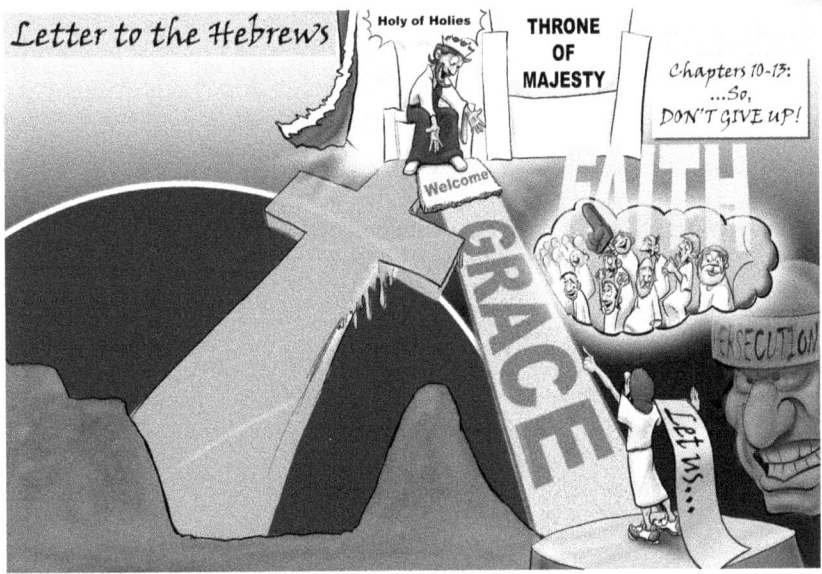

Week 12: Running the Race

- Read: Hebrews 12

Study Questions

1. Make a list of the things the author instructs the reader to do. (Let us...)

2. To whom does the phrase "cloud of witnesses" refer?

3. What do they have to do with running the race?

Faith that Transcends

4. What is it about Jesus that we are to consider? Why?

5. How are we to perceive difficult times in life? Why? What is your response to this notion? Why? What questions does it spark for you?

6. To what end are we to strive? (verse 14) Why?

7. What does bitterness do to a relationship?

HEBREWS

8. How might bitterness, sexual immorality and godlessness (literally meaning to profane or completely deny God or others) be related and hurtful toward the goal of living at peace with all people?

9. How is Esau an example of this? (you can find his story in Genesis 25)

10. What image of God do the people have as they looked up at the mountain in Exodus 19?

11. How is this image of God contrasted with the picture painted in Hebrews 12:22-24?

12. What point is the author making by comparing Jesus' blood with the blood of Abel? (that story is found in Genesis 4)

13. Instead of refusing Jesus, what attitude should we show toward him? Why?

HEBREWS

Food for Thought

"Running in the wrong cloud" (1-3)

You've heard the expression, "he's running with the wrong crowd." In verses 1-3 the author encourages the reader not to "run in the wrong cloud." In verse 1 we see that a great cloud of witnesses is "perikeimenon" lying around us. It encompasses us. It is, in a positive sense, like a thick fog. Perhaps a better analogy would be to say that it is like the air that surrounds us. It is outside of us, around us, and it permeates us. Then we see that there is another cloud that surrounds us as well. In the various English translations sin is said to "ensnare us" "entangled us" "so easily besets us." The Greek word is "euperistaton" and literally means "good-around-stands". The thing that ties these two words together is the prefix "peri" which means around. The witnesses are around us, and sin is around us. They are both like a cloud. Perhaps we can get a sense of the meaning here if we switch metaphors for a moment. Let's talk about the radio. Right now, where you sit, you are surrounded by hundreds of radio frequencies. They are coursing through your body. The only way that you can become conscious of them is if you have a radio receiver that is tuned into the correct frequency. If you want the country station, tune to 105.2. If you want the rock station, tune to 99.7. If you want to tune into the positive example and energy of the heroes of faith that have gone before you, then pay attention to them. If you want to be dragged down by negativity, bitterness, unforgiveness, hatred, etc. and have your energy sucked dry from you, then focus on that garbage. The choice is yours. Where's your radio tuned?

The point of living is to run the race marked out for us. This statement raises a huge question for us. What is the race? Where do we run? What are we supposed to do? This is the race of faith; it is the process of believing. But, as we discussed in the last chapter, it is not a blind faith. The answer is not in the Disneyism to simply "believe." Faith has an object. The race has a plan and a course. The course has been marked out by Jesus. He has told us how to live in His teaching. However, He did more than just tell us how to live. Jesus modeled it for us by His life, death, and resurrection. Jesus taught us to love God with all our heart and to love our neighbor. Then He did it. He obeyed God and lived in constant fellowship and obedience to God. Then, in the greatest miracle of all time, Jesus demonstrated the ultimate other-oriented love by giving Himself up to death. In doing this Jesus marked out the course and showed us how children of God live. They love. They give. They think of others as better than themselves. Then they die for the good of others. They place self aside and give recklessly. In so doing they demonstrate the very essence of God and sit down at the right hand of the Father.

The analogy of running a race that the author uses in this passage is both extremely helpful and full of dangerous pitfalls (as are all analogies). On the positive side, the analogy reminds us that life is a matter of focus. We need to fix our eyes on Jesus, not the sin, or the witnesses. Once we become distracted by our own fear, or our own selfishness, or by the accolades of those around us for doing a good job, we will lose sight of Jesus' model of selflessness and begin to run into the Kingdom of our own self. All we have to do is stay pointed in the right direction, keep believing, and keep "running."

This analogy falls down when we get too focused on the linear aspects of it. It is not a linear process of moving from point A to point B, as if there was a place where Jesus sits and we are to run to Him. The metaphor instructs us to be aware of the "how" Jesus ran His life. He did it through faith in God, in the presence of the witnesses, and with other-oriented love as the means by which He ran. He was not a driven, goal-oriented go-getter, trying to please God or earn favor by doing good. He was just the opposite. He took the goal that was His right -- the throne of Heaven -- and gave it up for us. It is in this demonstration of selflessness that He has saved the world. He invites us to set our eyes on His example and run in such a way that we embrace the energy of faith that is demonstrated by those who have gone before us, ignore the selfishness and self-defeating tendencies that try to blind and distract us, and live life in such a way that we become the conduit of God's other-oriented love to the world.

Storm clouds are good things, embrace the darkness (4-13)

Let's be honest. Most people don't really like pain. Pain hurts. Thunderstorms are nice to look at from the safety of a secure house, behind thick glass, snuggled in a warm blanket, but nobody likes being blasted with cold wind and thrashed around like a rag doll, fearing for your life. Yet, pain happens. In fact, pain happens on a regular basis. Now, let's be honest for a moment. When you read this passage it is quite possible that you felt some sense of skepticism creep up in your mind. There are many ways that you could read this section. Here are a few possibilities:

God likes to beat his kids. Hey, He's God, so quit your whining. You'll thank Him later, so drop and give me twenty!

or

You aren't good enough yet. You need to work harder if you want to be good. Every time you sin God is going to throw pain into your life to punish you. The reason you are suffering right now is because you have unconfessed sin in your life. The less sin you have the less suffering you will have. Someday you'll get it right and then you will experience the blessings of God and be healthy and stop suffering.

Both of these readings are problematic when held up against the overarching message of God's grace and love for His children. Perhaps there is an alternative perspective. A parent's job is to train a child. Similarly a coach's job is to train an athlete. The coach trains the athlete to execute a specific skill in an event. The parent's job is to train the child in matters of character and life skills so that they can survive and thrive in the adult world. Neither the parent nor the coach would ever want to be brutal or hurt the child for no reason. The motivation behind everything they do (in the ideal model of course) is the good of the child. As Mr. Miaggi trained the karate kid, sometimes there are periods of waxing on and waxing off that don't make sense and make the body hurt, but they are designed to shape the muscles and the character toward the desired goal. God is our perfect, divine parent who desires to form us into loving people who behave toward one another in the way that Jesus modeled for us. God does not want to hurt us, nor does He take pleasure in our pain. He doesn't necessarily send circumstances to us based upon our behavior in a direct one-to-one relationship. Perhaps, instead, He provides a model for us to deal with every circumstance in a way that causes us to grow. Circumstances are the discipline -- the training -- we need to become the children we were designed to be.

In life there are good times and bad times. The truth is that the value of circumstances is largely determined by the way in which we choose to perceive them. If we receive a boat load of money and use it to feed our own selfishness, then this circumstance is actually a painfully destructive event for us. However, if severe persecution brings us to a place of total dependence on God and the ability to forgive our assailant then that circumstance was the greatest blessing we could every receive. Put plainly, part of running the race of Jesus is to realize that every circumstance is as an opportunity to learn and to grow. Conversely, it is also an opportunity to dwell on the negative and feed a selfish and/or self-destructive pattern of thinking.

In the context of the letter to the Hebrews, the author is encouraging his readers to not give up. They were facing severe persecution (God's discipline) and were being tempted to turn away from Jesus. The author reminds them to not give up, but to embrace these present difficulties as a gift from God that will make them better people.

What are the circumstances in your life right now that could be easily interpreted as negative or difficult? Spend some time asking God how you might be able to tune into the "cloud of witnesses" and see how this same circumstance can teach you a valuable lesson in life that will empower you to love with Jesus' love.

Grace and Peace is the Goal (14-17)

The apostle Paul began many of his letters with the greeting "grace and peace to you." This was not just a nicety at the beginning of a letter. These two words hold the keys to running the Jesus race. We see it in this passage as the author instructs the readers to "live at peace with all men" and then to not "miss the grace of God." Isn't that what the whole gospel is about? The world is being torn apart by people hating each other and fighting with one another. People turn their backs on each other and on God. God is love. God is the bond that draws us all together. Jesus came to demonstrate that kind of love by completely swimming against the stream of human society and extending grace to His assailants. He didn't fight back or repay evil with evil. He repaid evil with love and forgiveness. What was the result of this kind of counter-intuitive behavior? Peace. As Paul taught us in Romans, because of Jesus, we are at peace with God. We have been reconciled to God. As we have learned in Hebrews, shrouded in Old Testament language, Jesus has paid the sin offering once and for all, thus allowing us entrance into the holy of holies. God does not condemn, He welcomes. This is the Good News, through grace there is peace.

Now, what is the opposite of grace and peace? Selfishness and strife. When I look at you and see you as an object either to be used for my own gratification or to be beaten away for my own protection, then I am living in Hell -- the opposite of the realm of grace and peace. Notice the things the author mentions that will destroy the peace in a community: bitterness, sexual immorality, and godlessness.

HEBREWS

Bitterness: the literal meaning of bitterness is something that is painful to the touch; something that repels you when you contact it. When water becomes bitter it ceases to be useful and becomes disgusting and unpalatable. When a person becomes bitter it can take on many forms. Essentially it is like milk going bad. The person's heart is poisoned and they can no longer see the good in anything. The root of bitterness can be planted through many different ways. A person can be offended or violated. A person can be disappointed by someone, or lose something significant. No matter what the cause, when bitterness begins to grow it begins to manifest in outbursts of anger, envy, gossip, sabotage, distrust, or depression. A bitter person lives with a double-edged sword. On the one hand they are sick and hurting and need desperately to be healed by the loving touch of another, but on the other hand their bitterness is unpalatable to those around them and no one wants to get near them. Thus, the bitterness cycle deepens with each passing rejection. A bitter soul in the midst of a community is like a cancer that will slowly sour the whole pot. It must be confronted and healed if the whole community is going to run the Jesus race and live in grace and peace.

Sexual immorality: Quite simply, sexual immorality is the objectification of the other. It is when one person looks at another person and says, "I want to look at you or touch you so that I can experience the kind of pleasure that I want. I want to use you as an object for my gain." Our sexuality is a gift from God. We were designed as men and women, sexually complementary creatures, so that, in the covenant of marriage, we could experience the deepest level of body/mind/spirit intimacy possible. However, the only way for sexual intimacy to be truly effective is for each party to look to the need of the other. In light of this definition it is even possible to have sexual immorality within the marriage relationship. If sex doesn't open up communication and other-focus, then it is simply a utilitarian act that is most likely meeting the needs of only one party at a time. Whenever sexual immorality is present in a community it tends to create a climate in which all people are objectified. A Jesus community should be one in which all members are looking out for the needs of the other and are willing to enter into self-disclosive levels of communication so that everyone can know and be known.

Godlessness: the Greek word is "bebalos" and it means "profane" or "that which has turned completely away from God." We must read this word in the context of 'godless like Esau." How was Esau godless? Simply put, Esau put his stomach ahead of everything else. He was hungry so he was willing to sell his birthright. At the root of it is selfishness and self-indulgence. When the community has selfish people, then people will get used up. Here is the great dilemma of living in a real-life community. Let's say that 80% of the people in a community are truly trying to live an other-oriented life, putting the needs of others above their own needs. Now let's say that the other 20% are living in a totally self-indulgent mode (godless). What's going to happen? The selfish people will suck every ounce of love and grace out of the others until everyone is dry. After all, we are all human and no one can survive without their own needs being met as well. To say that you are putting the needs of others above your own does not mean that you don't also have needs. In a community where everyone loves selflessly, then everyone's needs are also being met. But, in a community where only a few are being selfish, then all the love will be sucked into the black hole of their greedy and needy heart.

As you can see, these three things are community busters. They are enemies of the grace and peace that characterizes the Jesus race. So, how do we guard against these things? Do we throw out the brother that is infected, thus preserving our inner sanctum? Here's the irony. The answer is the same as the goal. We love them, unconditionally. We need to all admit that we are all infected by these three bugs to some level or another and we all need to be inoculated by the gracious love of God as it is demonstrated, first through Jesus, and then overflowing through each other in our community. If we start throwing each other out or managing each other's sin, then we will become agents of destruction and division in the body. Instead, it is our job to "fix our eyes on Jesus" and worry about loving according to His standard. When we enter into dialogue about who we really are and how we are really feeling and create a safe environment where we can open ourselves up, then the love of God is being demonstrated and we can shift from tuning into the cloud of sin that surrounds us and tune into the cloud of witnesses that surround us. Then, through the grace and peace of God, we can experience the healing and transformation that we need.

New Metaphors (18-24)

In this passage the author taps into a deeply rooted image for the Hebrew mind. The God who gave the law to Moses was the scary God of the mountain. Why was He this God? Because that is how the people wanted to perceive Him. Their hearts were closed to the idea of the infinite God. They lived in fear of God, so God was scary. Moses, on the other hand, was invited into the presence of God and felt courage to dialogue with God and even challenge Him. Yet, that image of God is not complete, or even a good one. Here, the author of Hebrews offers us an image of God that was made very clear through the ministry of Jesus. Here we see God as a beautiful, inviting, and joyous city that will provide us with all the things we need.

Both of these images are simply metaphors. God is not a cloud, a bolt of lightning, nor a city. In our day, one of the challenges for our culture is to discover metaphors for God that will convey the message of Jesus and connect to the hearts of this generation. What does grace and peace actually look like in our world. What is the vision of God's preferred future that we can share with the world as we invite all people into the race of Jesus?

Remember what Matters (25-29)

Here we end where we began. The word "refuse" is translating the Greek word "paraiteomai" and it literally means "to beg off" or "to ask to be excused and turn away from." In the beginning of this chapter the author said to look intently toward Jesus and not take your eyes off of him. Now he reminds us to not turn away from Jesus -- to refuse Him -- because if we do we will run right back into that cloud of sin and lose sight of the purpose of running.

… Faith that Transcends

HEBREWS

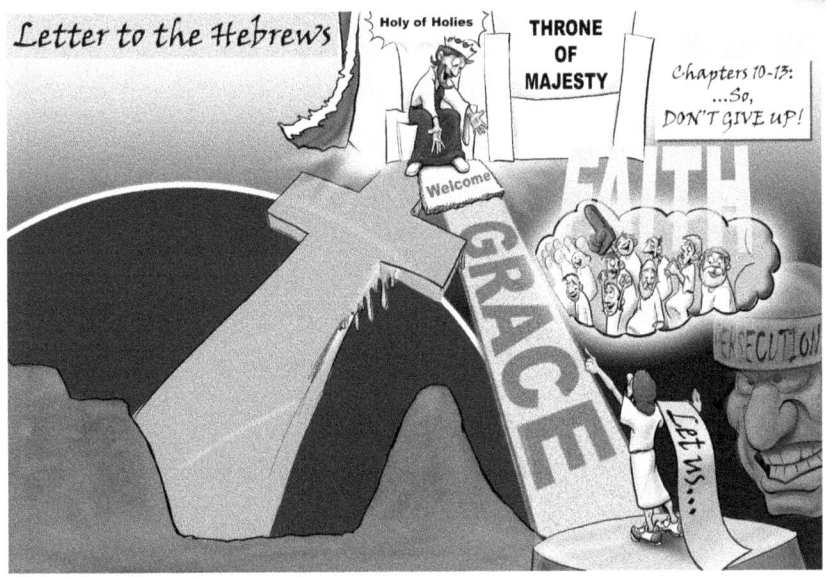

Lesson 13: Going Outside the City

- Read: Hebrews 13

Study Questions

1. As you read through this chapter, list all of the instructions the author gives to the reader (do this…; don't do this…., etc.)

2. As you reflect on the topics of these instructions, what area is God showing you that needs work in your life?

3. In verses 15-16, what kind of sacrifice is God looking for? Why?

4. What have you learned from the letter to the Hebrews that will help you in your relationship with God as you navigate life with others in the world?

HEBREWS

Food for Thought

Wrapping it up

Imagine the following scene. A doting mother watches as her son carries his bags out the door as he leaves for his first semester at college. As he throws the bags into the trunk she calls out to him, "Don't forget to brush! Be good! Don't stay up too late! Do your homework! Have fun! Don't forget to call!" Through tears she watches him drive away and hopes that he will be safe and remember all the things she worked so hard to teach him.

In many ways this is what the final chapter of Hebrews feels like. The author has poured his heart out to the Hebrews. He has been deeply concerned for their physical and spiritual well being in the face of extremely difficult circumstances. He has built a compelling theological case for why it is necessary for them to place their full trust in Jesus and not give in to the temptation to betray him at the hands of Roman Imperial pressure. Now the preaching is over and, as the hearers "drive away" from this message he seems to be calling out a hodge podge of instructions for their health and well being.

We can see this shift in the grammar of the passage. Up to this point whenever the author was giving instructions he would tend to serve up the salad and say "let us" do this and "let us" do that. For those of you who care, this is called the subjunctive mood. It has a humble sense of inclusive "us" as the author includes himself in the group that needs to do the things he is instructing. Now the mood changes to the imperative. This is the command voice. It comes from one person to another and says, "Do this!"

When we organize the chapter around the imperatives we can see the main topics.

A List of Imperatives

- ◇ Let brotherly love remain! (verse 1)
- ◇ Don't forget the love of the stranger (verse 2)
- ◇ Remember the prisoner (verse 3)

  Adjectives and nominatives (it is interesting to note that verses 4-6 are not in the imperative. Instead it is a string of statements that read as follows. While it is valid to translate them as instructions, it is also worth noting that the author does not state them in the imperative. Why? We're not sure... it's just an observation)

- marriage is valuable and
- the bed undefiled
- The manner is not loving silver
- being content in the present
- Scripture quotations -- God will be with us

the Imperatives continue...

- Remember your leaders (verse 7)
- Do not be carried along by various and strange teachings (verse 9)
- Do not forget to do good and to share (koinonia) (verse 16)
- Be persuaded by your leaders and submit to them (verse 17)
- Pray for us (verse 18)

A Final Message for Us

The author touches on many important topics in this grab bag of concluding remarks. Each one of them merits an entire book of commentary and practical application. He touches on the need to not just focus on loving your spiritual community but to also reach outside of the community -- to the "stranger" -- and love him as well. Then he talks about how important it is to keep the purity of marriage and the covenant within that relationship strong and undefiled. He talks about being content in the present circumstances by trusting that God will always supply your needs. Then he talks about the need to respect and follow your spiritual leaders in order to maintain peace and unity in the body and to be protected from being pulled back into the legalism of the "old ways."

Rather than write a small commentary on each of these topics, I would like to conclude our study together by focusing on the one section that most captivated my imagination. In verses 9-16 the author essentially summarizes the entire teaching of Hebrews and synthesizes it into a compelling challenge for his readers. As we read this section I think there is a message and a challenge for us as well. Let's look closely at this section.

Allow me to paraphrase this section in order to get at the heart of the meaning for the original reader, and then transpose that meaning into a possible reading for the state of the church in our world today.

HEBREWS

Don't get sucked back into the old way of doing things and get tripped up by that kind of teaching. There are a lot of powerful religious leaders who focus all of their energy on "doing it right" in the Temple. They honestly believe that it is all about getting the sacrifices right and being ceremonially clean. Remember, we serve Jesus. He showed us that all of that stuff means nothing if it is not flowing from a humble and thankful heart. God invites us to tap into His grace and realize that He loves us and wants to transform us from the inside out. When we are transformed from the inside, then we will overflow with the kind of sacrifice God truly desires -- humble thanksgiving, praise, and authentic love for all people.

Remember, however, that this kind of thinking is going to get you into a lot of trouble. It got Jesus into trouble. The religious leaders did not want to hear His teaching. They were so opposed to Him that they killed Him for it. They took Him outside the city walls, to the place of disgrace, and killed Him like a common criminal. There is a great analogy in that. The only sacrifice that actually mattered was one that was "outside" the norms of proper religiosity. It was offered in humility and disgrace. To be a true follower of Jesus we need to be willing to be misunderstood by the established power structures of religion and go "outside" the city to where Jesus is. There Jesus invites all people, great and small, to join Him in humble worship of God through the service of all people.

The message of Hebrews was a reminder that the "Good News" that Jesus proclaimed was a call to take a radical stance of humble love that challenged the very core of established Jewish doctrine and practice. Jesus was a Jewish man and the Jewish Messiah, but He fulfilled His Jewish mission by being very "un-Jewish." He tore down the humanly constructed doctrines of "sin management" and external behavior modification through fear and intimidation and proposed a new way of being.

The message of Jesus has not changed. Every generation needs to hear it again. It is the perpetual human tendency to take the mysterious encounter of "God with us" and lock it into a code and system of do's and don'ts. To quote a cliché, we love to put God in our box. Then we worship our box. The doctrinal box that we build leads us to believe that we have the definitive word on who

God is and how God functions in the universe, and that everyone who disagrees with us is wrong. Our box becomes "a holy city' in which those who agree with us live and those who disagree are kept out. For every generation, Jesus comes to the box to break down its walls, only to be cast outside the city and discarded as a criminal. And in every generation He calls to all who will listen to join Him in that place of humility and disgrace to worship God with the humbled heart of a servant.

The challenge for us as followers of Jesus in the 21st century is to ask, "What is the Good News of Jesus?" What is the message that Jesus has for us? What is Jesus asking us to focus our time and energy on in the church? Should we focus on doing church the "right way?" Should we focus on having a "correct doctrinal statement" and then judge everyone according to their agreement or disagreement with that statement? Should we spend our time condemning the sin of the "world" when we can't even get it straight in our own homes? Should we erect a "holy city" that has thick walls in which only the 'righteous' and "elect" can live? Or, is Jesus calling us to love the stranger? Is He calling us to go outside the city, to the garbage dump, and love the world the way He loved the world? We want to build the city and get it "right" because we want to honor a Holy God by becoming holy people. That is a noble motive. Yet, perhaps it is only when we are willing to go out to the dump and leave the "rightness" of our city that WE built, that we can actually see God, be purified by Him, and offer the kind of sacrifices that God truly desires from us. He desires us to love each other just like Jesus did.

So, as we leave this study of Hebrews, I hope that you have been challenged and encouraged. As the author to his readers did then, so do I now; I pray that you will know God, walk humbly in the Grace of Jesus, and love both your brother and the stranger equally. Please pray for me, as I continue my journey in the Grace of God and seek to know how I can be used by Him and for Him in whatever way I can. All praise and glory to Him.

More titles from Vibble Books

The Overflow Principle
v7-week group study. This study explores what it means to love God with a whole heart -- Mind, Spirit, Body -- and to love your neighbor as yourself.

The Life of Jesus
a 15-week, 5-day per week study that will guide you through all four Gospels, woven together in a chronological presentation of Jesus' life.

Acts
a 12-week, 5-day per week study that will guide you through the book of Acts. This is the story of the first generation of Jesus-folowers as they spread from Jerusalem throughout the Roman Empire.

Paul's Letters
a 16-week, 5-day per week guide through all of the letters that Paul wrote both to churches and individuals. Through these letters we have a model of how to contextualize Jesus' message for specific cultural issues.

View all the titles at www.vibblebooks.com

www.ingramcontent.com/pod-product-compliance
Ingram Content Group UK Ltd.
Pitfield, Milton Keynes, MK11 3LW, UK
UKHW022224230426
12048UKWH00016BA/1052